WRITE PERFECT LETTERS FOR ANY OCCASION

by

R. Emil Neuman

WRITE PERFECT LETTERS
FOR ANY OCCASION

ISBN 0-9614924-5-7

Published by
United Research Publishers
Box 2344
Leucadia, CA 92024

Printed in U.S.A.

CONTENTS

BUSINESS MODELS

SOCIAL MODELS

INTRODUCTION

You no longer have to waste time and energy writing letters from scratch — searching for the perfect words, agonizing over the best way to express yourself in writing. Now you can create perfect letters in just minutes!

This book, *Write Perfect Letters For Any Occasion,* contains hundreds of letters written by top professionals. You can copy these letters word-for-word, or use them as guides to write your own letters. In minutes, you'll be creating perfect letters — making the right impressions, getting the results you want.

Here are some of the key topics covered in this book:

- **How to make letters look attractive.** This book shows you how to select the right paper, proper letterheads and envelopes, spacing, width of margins and folding. Attractive looking letters make a good first impression!

- **How to write business letters.** This book contains dozens of business letters such as inquiries, requests, asking for prices and samples, ordering products, complaint letters, requests for payment, announcements, sales letters and much more. Well written business letters get action!

- **How to write personal letters.** This book shows you how to create hard-to-write letters such as letters of sympathy, illness notes, letters of congratulations, notes of apology, condolences, asking for advice, school excuses and much more.

- **How to write social letters.** This book shows you countless examples of social letters such as gift notes, invitations to luncheons and dinners, announcements, formal invitations, broken appointments, last minute cancellations, children's parties and much more.

- **How to avoid costly mistakes in English.** This book quickly shows you proper punctuation — when to use the period, comma, semi-colon, colon, exclamation point, the dash, hyphen, parenthesis, the apostrophe and quotation marks. The book also covers proper capitalization and lists the 200 most commonly misspelled words.

In addition to showing you hundreds of model letters, the book gives you the tools needed to write your own letters from scratch. The book gives you a strategy for creating your own terrific letter — from devising a plan, creating the all important first sentence to selecting the proper complimentary close. You'll discover how to make your letters clear and understandable by keeping language simple and avoiding unnecessary words.

I hope you enjoy the book and I wish you the very best.

The Author

Chapter 1

How To Write
A Good Letter

Aside from the fact that a letter should be clear, smooth, coherent and all the things you learn in a letter-writing course, one factor rises above all else. The letter should achieve the results intended by the writer. If this does not happen, the letter falls short of being totally successful.

Every letter should have a purpose — a reason for being written. The main thrust of the letter should be centered around that purpose. Always have the main purpose in mind before you start to create a letter.

Start With A Plan

Examples of most letters you want to write can be found in this book either in the Business Letter or Social Letter section. But if you want to create your own letter from scratch, there are a few simple things you should do before you start writing. These are:

1. Think about what you want to say and pinpoint your main purpose or thrust of the letter.

2. Put your main ideas into key words or phrases and jot them down in order of importance.

3. Visualize your reader and establish a tone for the letter. This is easy if you know the person. If not, try to think what the person would be like.

If you are answering a friend's letter, review what he or she said so you can answer questions or comment on what they said. Likewise, if you're replying to a letter requesting information, review the letter to be sure you are answering all the questions asked.

The First Paragraph

The first paragraph is probably the most important part of your letter. Here is where you grasp the reader's attention and set the stage for the rest of the letter. The first paragraph is where you affect the reader's mood and where he or she decides whether or not to read the entire letter.

The first paragraph generally states the main message of the letter and is from where the remainder of the letter unfolds. The reader should not have to plow through a lot of sentences before he knows what the letter is about. The purpose or thrust of the letter should "pop out" at the reader.

Even a letter to a close friend should have a lively first paragraph such as, "I haven't heard from you in a while, Terry. How are you?" Don't waste this important first paragraph on stale standard phrases such as, "With regard to your letter dated ..."

Avoid Unnecessary Words

There is nothing wrong with a long letter if that's what is required to convey your message. Sometimes it is a good idea to place in your letter additional words to add friendliness and warmth to your correspondence. That's fine.

Unnecessary words are words that clutter the message of the letter. Unnecessary words do not add a single thing to the message and, in fact, detract from the message of the letter.

Examples of Improving Letters by Eliminating Unnecessary Words

If you want to improve your letter-writing, start eliminating the unnecessary words in every sentence. For example:

Letter With Unnecessary Words

Dear Mr. Adams:

With reference to your letter of request for credit with our firm, dated April 16, we have carefully reviewed all the credit information you sent us and have concluded that we will be able to grant you a line of credit in the amount of $3,000.

Sincerely,

With Unnecessary Words Deleted

Dear Mr. Adams:

We are pleased to grant you a $3,000 line of credit.

Sincerely,

Notice that the first version has 43 words while the revised version contains only 11 words. A full 32 words were eliminated without affecting the clarity of the message. In fact, the revised version is much easier to understand with the unnecessary words eliminated. Another example follows.

Letter With Unnecessary Words

Gentlemen:

In looking through your fall *Health and Fitness* catalog, I noticed that you carry two types of zinc products in the 100 tablet size bottles. One product is 50 mg of zinc shown on page 14, and the other is 100 mg shown on page 26.

I am interested in a 50 mg bottle of 100 but I don't know whether the zinc is zinc gluconate or zinc ascorbate. I prefer the zinc gluconate over zinc ascorbate.

If the 50 mg of zinc is zinc gluconate, then send me one bottle of 100 and charge my Visa number shown above. Thank you so much.

Cordially yours,

Unnecessary Words Deleted:

Gentlemen:

If the 50 mg zinc listed in your fall catalog is zinc gluconate, send me a bottle of 100 and charge my Visa.

Cordially yours,

There are a number of unnecessary, repetitive or roundabout phrases that can be streamlined to improve your letters:

Wordy	Simplified
for the purpose of	for
subsequent to	after
in the event that	if
despite the fact that	though
reduce to a minimum	minimize
sells at a price of	sells for
at a later date	later
at the present time	now
due to the fact that	since
inasmuch as	since
in order to	to

Wordy	Simplified
in the event that	if
in the normal course	normally
in the very near future	soon
in view of the fact	because
of the order of magnitude	about
prior to	before
pursuant to our agreement	as we agreed
will you be kind enough to	please
enclosed please find	enclosed
at an early date	soon
at all times	always
until such time as	until
in the course of	during
it is requested that you	please
in compliance with your request	as requested
costs the sum of	costs
we regret to advise	we are sorry
keep in mind the fact that	remember that
until such time as you are in a position	when you are able
being sold at a price of	sells for

Keep Language Simple

Many people believe that the use of big words is a sign of intelligence. Accordingly, they use a big word not recognized by many when a more commonly used word would make the correspondence more clear and understandable. Nobody is going to question the virtue of a rich vocabulary. And there are many useful big words for which a more common substitute is not available. But there is no excuse for purposely using a big word when an alternative would make your message more clear.

Here are a few examples of where more commonly used words are preferred over big words:

Big Word	More Commonly Recognized (Preferred)
endeavor	try
feasible	possible
equitable	fair
ascertain	discover
initiate	begin
consummate	complete
concur	agree
procure	get
verification	proof
reiterate	repeat
subsequently	after
tardy	late

Be Positive

Remember that a letter is a substitute for a face-to-face visit. Someone once said that a good letter sounds like the writer "put himself in the envelope" and then "pops out" to express his message to the reader.

If you were having a face-to-face meeting with the reader, you would want to put your best foot forward. You would want to emphasize the positive and be constructive.

Well, the same applies to letters.

Examples of Negative and Positive Letters

If you want to improve your letter writing, start emphasizing the positive.

For example:

Negative Letter

Dear Mr. Jacobs:

I am so sorry to inform you that we are temporarily out of stock of the blue aviator-style flight jackets and will not be able to fill your order at the present time.

We have placed another order with our supplier but it will be another five days before we receive the jackets.

We are very sorry for any inconvenience this may have caused you.

Sincerely yours,

Positive Letter

Dear Mr. Jacobs:

Thank you for ordering our aviator-style flight jacket.

The blue color you ordered is so popular, our inventory is sold out.

We have ordered more from our supplier and expect delivery within five days. Your blue jacket will be rushed to you the moment we receive our new supply.

Mr. Jacobs, I'm sure you will be very satisfied with your handsome aviator-style flight jacket. Thank you so much for your patience.

Sincerely yours,

Notice how the first version contains several negative phrases such as, "I am so sorry," and "not be able to," which give the entire letter a negative overtone. The revised letter has a more positive tone and would result in fewer order cancellations. Another example follows.

Negative Letter

Dear Nancy,

I deeply regret that I will not be able to accept your invitation to spend the weekend with you and Bill at your cottage. Unfortunately, I'll be out of town that weekend.

Maybe you could invite me some other time when I'm not so busy. Thanks anyway for the invitation.

As Ever,

Positive Letter

Dear Nancy,

Your welcome invitation to join you and Bill at your cottage this weekend came this morning. Thanks so much for asking me. You know I always enjoy your company.

I would love to come, but I'll be in Denver that weekend on business. I made this commitment over seven months ago.

It was so thoughtful of you for thinking of me, Nancy. Let's keep in touch and get together another time real soon.

As Ever,

Both letters clearly convey the message that Terri won't be able to accept the invitation. But which refusal letter would you rather receive?

Chapter 2

How To Avoid Mistakes In English

Mistakes in English can leave an unfavorable impression on the reader and impact the overall effectiveness of a letter.

The most common mistakes made in letters relate to punctuation and spelling. The purpose of punctuation is to make writing easier to read and interpret. Punctuation gives expression and emphasis to writing the same way gestures, pauses and raising the voice give emphasis to speaking. Knowing the use of basic punctuation will help you create better letters.

Misspelled words can take on a meaning different than what the writer intended. That's why it's important to look up the spelling in a dictionary when in doubt. Most people have difficulty spelling the same troublesome words.

Below you will find a quick guide to basic punctuation and a list of the 200 most commonly misspelled words.

The Period (.)

Use a period:

- After a declarative or imperative sentence and after indirect questions:

    Everyone should drive carefully. (declarative)

    Learn how to drive carefully. (imperative)

    She asked if the snow was shoveled. (indirect question)

- After most abbreviations:

    Ph.D., U.S., Mr., Mrs., Dr., A.M., P.M., etc.

- Three periods (ellipsis) ... are used to show the omission of one or more words within a quotation.

  "I believe in absolute freedom of speech ... anyone who doesn't agree should be silenced."

The Comma (,)

Use a comma:

- To separate the name of a city from a state:

  Los Angeles, California

- To separate the name of a person from the rest of the sentence:

  Sally, wash my car.

- To separate one part of a sentence from another:

  Mr. Wilson, the accountant, will be here at noon.

- To separate introductory words and phrases:

  No, I did not go shopping.

  If you have the shirt in blue, send me one.

- To set off a direct quotation from the rest of a sentence:

  Joe said, "Let's have dinner."

- To separate words in a series:

  Jack is healthy, wealthy, smart and wise.

- To separate two parts of a sentence connected by a conjunction:

  She likes rock music, but I like jazz.

- To separate the day of the week from the month, and the day of the month from the year:

  Tuesday, May 10

  June 7, 1999

- After the salutation in a personal letter:

  Dear Sam,

The Semicolon (;)

Use the semicolon:

- To separate parts of a compound sentence when the conjunction and comma are omitted:

  Close the door; it's cold in the house.

- To separate two independent clauses joined by a conjuction and already containing commas:

  Once Raymond got the job, he traveled to Detroit, Boston and San Diego; but he missed home so much, he quit the job.

- To separate a series of items that already contain commas:

  I will be traveling to Alpena, Michigan; Tempe, Arizona; Atlanta, Georgia; Dallas, Texas; and Willow, California.

The Colon (:)

Use a colon:

- To introduce a number of items that are to follow:

  Success in life requires the following: hard work, common sense and luck.

- To introduce a long quotation:

  Robert Owens once said:

    "We are all brothers sharing together a brief moment of life, seeking only to live out our lives with purpose and happiness, winning what satisfaction and fulfillment we can."

- To separate hours from minutes:

  9:20 PM

- After the salutation in business correspondence:

  Dear Mr. Barber:

The Dash (—)

Use the dash:

- To indicate a sudden break or abrupt change in thought:

    He said — and no one can contradict him — "The battle is lost."

- To obtain a pause before an important word at the end of a sentence:

    The whole mess — stinks!

- To indicate an unfinished statement:

    The little girl asked, "Is daddy going to —"
    "No," interrupted the mother.

The Exclamation Point (!)

The exclamation point is used to indicate surprise, admiration, appeal, incredulity or other strong emotions:

    He acknowledged the error!
    How beautiful!
    What!
    He shouted, "All aboard!"

The Hyphen (-)

Use the hyphen:

- To join two or more words serving as a single adjective *before* a noun:

    the bluish-green ocean

    sugar-covered raisins

    the thirty-one-year-old singer

However, the hyphen is omitted when the modifier follows the noun:

    The ocean is a bluish green color.

The raisins, which were sugar coated, tasted great.

The singer is thirty-one years old.

The hyphen is also omitted after an adverb ending in "ly":

a freshly prepared salad

a hopelessly lost cause

- With compound numbers from twenty-one to ninety-nine and with fractions:

    twenty-one

    ninety-eight

    one-fourth

- To avoid ambiguity or an awkward union between the prefix and root or suffix and root:

    re-creation

    semi-independent

    shell-like

- With the prefixes self-, all-, ex-, half-, great-, quarter-, and with the suffix -elect:

    ex-priest, self-made, all-purpose, great-uncle, senator-elect

- When a capital letter is joined with a noun:

    H-bomb

    X-ray

    U-turn

Parenthesis ()

Use parenthesis:

- To enclose nonessential explanations:

    Young adults are not allowed to drink until age 21 (18 in a few states) yet, they are allowed to fight at age 18.

- To enclose figures that are written out:

    A check for fifty dollars ($50) is enclosed.

- To enclose numbers or letters used to enumerate a series of items:

  The three main economic systems in the world today are (1) capitalism, (2) socialism and (3) communism.

The Apostrophe (')

Use the apostrophe:

- For singular nouns and plural nouns not ending in "s" to designate ownership or possession:

  man's

  girl's

  women's

- For plural nouns that end in "s" to show ownership or possession:

  visitors', babies', brothers'

- To show the omission of a letter or letters in a contraction:

  can't (for cannot)

  don't (for do not)

  I'm (for I am)

Quotation Marks (" ")

Use quotation marks:

- To enclose a direct quote:

  He said, "It's going to rain."

  When more than one paragraph is quoted, quotation marks are placed before each paragraph and at the close of the final paragraph only.

- To indicate titles of short stories, magazine articles, poems, etc.:

  I wrote a poem entitled "Call For Freedom" which was published in *Jet* magazine.

Titles of books, magazines and newspapers are italicized when printed and underlined when typed or handwritten. Using capitals for all letters is also acceptable for printed or typewritten titles.

- To enclose slang expressions, misnomers, coined words or ordinary words used in an arbitrary way:

    His report was "bunk."

    It was a "gentlemen's agreement."

    The "invisible government" is responsible.

    George Herman "Babe" Ruth

Capitalization

Capitalize the following:

- The first word in every sentence.

- The first word in a direct quotation:

    She said, "Hold the ball firmly."

- The days of the week, the months and holidays.

- The names of religious groups, political parties, races and languages:

Catholic	Lutheran
Indian	Oriental
Democrat	Republican
Latin	English

- Titles when used with proper names:

Queen Mary	Uncle Willy
President Allen	Chairman Albert

- North, South, East, West and Northwest, etc. when they refer to parts of the country or world, rather than a general direction.

31

- Persons, organizations, institutions, places, streets, buildings, parks, etc.

Joseph Perry	Elm Street
Cancer Association	Sears Tower
Orange Computer Company	Hines Park
Detroit	Rough River
California	Lake Murray

- Proper nouns and proper adjectives:
  Yale
  Scotland
  Abraham Lincoln
  They drank Italian wine.
  We had Japanese beer for lunch.

Guide To Correct Spelling

Of the thousands of words in the English language, only about 200 give people trouble in spelling. Listed below are the most commonly misspelled words:

absence	amateur	benefiting
accept	appearance	buoyant
accident	argument	business
accidentally	around	busy
accommodate	athletic	capital
acknowledgment	auxiliary	career
acquaint	beginning	catalog
acquaintance	believe	cemetery
across	believed	certain
affect	beneficial	character
aggravate	benefit	chief
all right	benefited	choose

chosen
coming
commit
commitment
committed
committee
committing
competition
complete
comptroller
conscientious
conscious
consensus
convenience
convenient
coolly
council
counsel
criticize
criticism
deceive
decide
decision
definite
descent
descendant, *or*
descendent
describe
description
desert
dessert
develop

difference
different
dining
disappear
disappoint
dividend
doesn't
don't
during
effect
eighth
embarrass
environment
equipment
equipped
escape
exaggerate
excellent
excite
excitement
exciting
exercise
existence
experiment
familiar
fascinate
February
finally
foreign
foreigners
forth
forty

four
friend
glamorous
glamour
government
grammar
grievance
hadn't
height
hero
heroes
heroine
humor
humorous
image
imaginary
imagination
imagine
immediate
immediately
individual
interest
interested
it's (contraction)
its
judgment
knowledge
knowledgeable
laboratory
latter
literature
lonely

loose
lose
losing
maintenance
marriage
marries
marry
meant
mischievous
monetary
municipal
necessary
necessity
noticeable
occasion
occasionally
occur
occurred
occurrence
occurring
o'clock
omitted
opinion
opportunity
parallel
parliament
performance
perhaps
personal
personnel
pleasant
possess

precede
prejudice
president
principal
principle
probably
proceed
professor
promissory
promotional
pronunciation
prophecy
prophesy
purchasable
quiet
quite
receive
recommend
referred
regrettable
relieve
responsibility
restaurant
rhythm
salable, *or*
saleable
schedule
seize
sense
separate
shining
similar

simplify
society
speech
stationary
stationery
stop
stopped
stopping
strength
studied
studies
study
studying
succeed
success
successful
superintendent
supersede
surprise
technicality
tendency
than
then
their
there
they're
thousandth
to
together
too
tragedy
transferred

transient
tries
tried
truly
two
until
villain
Wednesday
weird
where
whether
woman
writ
writer
writing
written
yield
you're
your

Chapter 3

Business Letters

Whether you are operating your business out of your home or work for a large corporation, business correspondence is an important business tool.

Business correspondence can tell a lot about your business. People often judge a business by the quality of its letters. A well-written letter that gets your point of view across effectively can get you that needed loan. A clear, concise letter to a supplier can get you that needed line of credit. A well-written response to a customer complaint may keep a good customer buying from your firm. A poorly written letter may result in the loss of a customer as well as damaging word-of-mouth publicity.

A much overlooked purpose of letters is the record they provide for transactions and agreements. This written record becomes very important when memories fail to recall specific details and disputes arise. Referring to past letters may reveal what was agreed, when an order was placed, what was ordered, and the promised delivery date. The facts can refresh recollections and allow parties to come to an amicable understanding.

On the other hand, not writing good letters can result in heated disputes, additional confusion, bad feelings and even court actions.

Selecting Stationery

The paper and envelopes used in business correspondence are called stationery. The paper you select is very important and can have a significant impact on the success of your letter. Letters typed on low-quality paper may cause someone to ignore your letter or read it with skepticism. This does not mean that you have to spend a lot of money for the highest quality paper, yet this is no place to skimp.

You should use good quality bond. The paper should look good and feel good. Typed characters and signatures should contrast neatly and you should be able to make corrections that are not easily detectable by the reader.

The most commonly used paper is 8½ x 11 inches and 20 pounds in weight. The greater the weight, the thicker the paper. Some firms use high quality 24 pound paper. For inter-office correspondence, 16 pound paper is often used. (The paper weight is derived from the weight of 500 17" x 22" sheets).

Most paper is made from a combination of wood and cotton fiber, with the cotton varying between 25 and 75 percent. The most expensive paper is made entirely from cotton fiber. Here again, a good medium quality paper will do fine for most businesses.

Selecting The Letterhead

Your stationery should have a letterhead printed on it. The letterhead should be simple and dignified. Old-fashioned letterheads were often ornate with a considerable amount of printed information.

Letterheads should be attractive and clearly project the image you want your business to have. The letterhead should contain the business name, address, telephone number and other ways to contact the firm, such as FAX numbers. Optional items are a brief description of the business or when it was founded.

Only the first page of a letter contains the letterhead. All other pages should be plain and the same color.

Generally, envelopes should match the paper in color, weight and quality. The number 10 envelopes fits the standard 8½ x 11 inch paper.

Making Letters Look Attractive

Once you have selected appropriate stationery, the attractiveness of your letter is largely a matter of spacing of the lines, margins and folding the letter. Of course, letters should be free from smudges, noticeable erasures and blots. Business letters should always be neat, attractive, dignified and businesslike.

Spacing

Most letters are single-spaced with double spaces between paragraphs. Letters that are short can be double-spaced, with triple spaces between paragraphs. Double spaces can be used between paragraphs when the paragraphs are indented.

Margins

Letters have margins at the top and bottom, and on both sides. The width of these margins varies with the length of the letter. Longer letters have narrower margins than shorter letters. The width of left and right margins should be at least one inch.

Margins on the top and bottom should be equal. When your letter is a full page, the top margin should start about one-and-one-half inches below the letterhead. When your letter is shorter, the top margin can be deeper as necessary. The bottom margin should be roughly the same as the top to give the letter an attractive, balanced look.The second page as well as subsequent pages of the letter should have the same margins as the first page. Of course, the last page will have the same top and side margins but the bottom margin is determined by the size of the letter.

Business letters should always be written on one side only.

Folding The Letter

The standard letter-size sheet, 8½ x 11 inches, fits into a standard number 10 envelope and should be folded as follows:

1. Fold the lower third of the letter up over the typed side of the letter.

2. Fold the upper third of the letter down over the lower folded part of the letter.

3. Insert the letter into the envelope with the upper folded edge sliding into the back of the envelope first.

Be sure the edges are even when folding the letter.

The Essential Parts
Of A Business Letter

Every business letter should consist of six essential parts. These are:

1. The heading
2. The inside address
3. The salutation
4. The body of the letter
5. The closing
6. The signature

Each part will be discussed later in this chapter.

The Heading

The heading consists of the sender's name and address and the date the letter was written. Since your printed stationery will already have the company's name and address, you'll only have to type in the date. The date will be either flush left or flush right, depending on the style of the letter. The heading makes it easier for the reader to reply to your letter.

The Inside Address

The inside address contains the recipient's name, title, company name and address. The inside address should be the same as it appears on the reader's own letterhead. It should be at least two lines below the heading.

The Salutation

The word salutation comes from the verb "to salute" or to greet. The salutation should be two spaces below the inside address. The salutation normally says, "Dear Mr. Jones," or "Dear Mrs. Smith." Always capitalize the first word of the salutation as well as names and titles. Use the recipient's first name if you know him well. Always place a colon after the salutation.

In cases where you're not sure of the recipient's name, use "To Whom It May Concern," or "Dear Sir," or Dear Madam."

The Body

The body is the main part of the letter and contains the message you want to convey to the reader. The body of the letter can be only one paragraph or as many paragraphs as needed to convey your message. The body should begin two lines below the salutation.

The Complimentary Closing

The complimentary closing is where you say farewell to the reader. It is two spaces below the body and is either flush left or centered, depending on the style of letter. Only the first word of the complimentary closing is capitalized. A comma always follows the close.

There are many options for the complimentary closing and you should use the one you feel most comfortable with.

Some commonly used forms of complimentary closings are:

Yours truly,

Yours very truly,

Very truly yours,

Sincerely,

Sincerely yours,

Yours sincerely,

Very sincerely yours,

Respectfully,

Yours respectfully,

Respectfully yours,

Cordially,

Cordially yours,

Yours cordially,

Each complimentary closing implies a varying degree of friendship and formality. Your best choice is the one most appropriate for your purpose. For example, you wouldn't use "Cordially yours" to someone you are suing. Nor would you use "Respectfully yours" to a clerk or casual business acquaintance.

The Signature

The name of the person writing the letter is typed four spaces below the complimentary close with the writer's signature in the blank space. All business letters should be signed in ink. The writer's title is normally typed after the name or immediately below. This is optional, depending on the image you want to portray and your relationship with the reader.

When the writer is not available to sign the letter, sometimes a secretary or another employee signs the letter. In this situation, the writer's name is signed with that person's initials immediately below.

It is customary to type the letter writer's and typist's initials two lines below the writer's name, flush left. The writer's initials are typed in all capitals, while the typists are typed in lower case with a slash or colon separating them.

Styles of Business Letters

There are several different styles of business letters that are commonly used in business. It is customary for a business to use just one particular style. The most widely used style is the block style. Examples of the different styles of business letters in general use today are shown on the following pages.

Full Block Style

Letterhead
Xxxx Xxxxxxxx Xx
(xxx) xxx-xxx

Date

Inside Address
xxxx Xxxxxxxx Xx
Xxxxxxxxxxxx, XX xxxxx

Salutation:

Every line of each paragraph is flush left. XXX
XXXXX XXX X XXXXXX XXXXXX X
XXXXXXX X XXXX XXX XXXXX. XXX
XXXXXXX XXXX XXX XXX XXXXXX.

X XXXXXX XXXXXXX XXX XXX. XXXX
XXXXX XXX XXXXX. XXXX XXXX X XX
XXXXXXXXXX. XXXXX XXX XX. X XX
XXXXX XXXXX XXXXX.

XX XXX X XXXX XXXXX XXXX. X XXX
XXXXXXX XXX X X XXXXX.

Complimentary Closing,

Name
Title

Enclosure

Block Style

Letterhead
xxxx Xxxxxxxx Xx
(xxx) xxx-xxx

Date

Inside Address
xxxx Xxxxxxxx Xx
Xxxxxxxxxxxx, XX xxxxx

Salutation:

The first sentence of each paragraph is indented.
XXXX XXX XXX XXXXXXXXXX. XXXXX X
XX. X XXX. X XXXXXXX XXXXXX XXXX.

There is a double-space between each paragraph.
XXXXXXX. XXXXXX XXXXX XXX XXXXX.
XXX XXX XXXXXXXXXX. XXXXX XXX XX.
XXXXX. XXX XXXXXXX XXXX XXX XXX
XXXXX XXXXX XXXXX.

The complimentary closing and signature are flush
right. XX XXX X XXXX XXXXX XXXX. XXXXX
XXX XX. X XXX XXXXXXX XXX X X XXXXX.

Complimentary closing,

Name
Title

Enclosure

Semi-Block Style

Letterhead
xxxx Xxxxxxxx Xx
(xxx) xxx-xxx

Date

Inside Address
xxxx Xxxxxxxx Xx
Xxxxxxxxxxxx, XX xxxxx

Salutation:

    The date line is flush left. XX XXXXX XXXX. XXX XXXXXXXXXX. XXXXX XXX XX. XXXXXX XXXXXX X XXX. X XXXXXXX XXXXXX XXXX.

    Paragraphs are indented and double spaced. X XXXXXXXXX. XXXXXX XXXXX XXX XX XXXXX XXXXX XXXXX.

    The closing and signature are centered. XXX XXXXXXX XXX X X XXXXX. XXXXXXX X XXX XXX XXXXXXXXXX. XXXXX XXX XX.

Complimentary closing,

Name
Title

Enclosure

Indented Style

Letterhead
xxxx Xxxxxxxx Xx
(xxx) xxx-xxx

Date

Inside Address
xxxx Xxxxxxxx Xx
Xxxxx, XX xxxxx

Salutation:

The date line starts at the center of the page and each line is indented five spaces from the line above.

X XXXXXX XXXXXXX XXX XXX. XXXX XXXX XXX XXX XXXXXXXXXX. XXXXX XX. XXXXXX XXXXX XXX XXXXX. XXXX XXXX X XXXX XXX XXXXX. XXX XXXX XXXX XXX XXX XXXXXXXXXX. XXXXX XX. X XXXX XXXXX XXXXX XXXXX.

XX XXX X XXXX XXXXX XXXX. XXXXXX XXXX XXX XXX XXXXXXXXXX. XXXXX XX. X XXX XXXXXXX XXX X X XXXXX.

Complimentary closing,

Name
Title

Enclosure

Business
Models

The business letters in this book are the most common and useful types of business letters. Each letter is well constructed and written in language currently in use. They will prove their effectiveness in business situations time and time again. These letters will get the results you want and make the right impressions.

When you need a specific type of correspondence, simply refer to the table of contents and select the appropriate letter. You can copy the letter word-for-word or use it as a guide to write your own letters. Sometimes a simple change of a word or two can "custom tailor" the letter to suit your needs. Other times you may wish to take a sentence or two from one letter and additional sentences from other letters, creating your own letter.

Chapter 4

Letters of Announcement

Letters of announcement often take the form of a news release. A news release format adds an air of importance to the letter.

An announcement letter is often used for such things as the appointment of a new employee, notice of a price increase (or decrease), change of delivery policy, or new address.

Letters of announcement generally should be brief, yet cover all essential facts. When announcing changes in policies or prices, the specific reasons should be covered and explain how the change may benefit the reader.

Notice of Price Increase

Dear Mr. Rollens:

Due to the increase in raw material costs, we must unfortunately raise the cost of our merchandise to you.

We have avoided raising our prices for as long as possible, but we can no longer prolong the inevitable. We have enclosed our new price list which goes into effect on May 15. Any orders placed before that date will be honored at the lower prices.

We wish to thank you for your valued business and hope you will understand the necessity for this price increase.

Sincerely,

Notice of Price Increase

Dear Mr. Weasle:

While we have been able to hold the line on prices for five years, we now find it necessary to increase prices slightly due to the rising cost of labor and legislated fringe benefits. Starting July 1, we must raise prices on all jewelry items a small one percent. Our revised price list is enclosed and I'm sure you'll agree the increases are very modest.

We are doing all we can to keep costs down and we look forward to serving you in the future.

Sincerely,

Change In Delivery Policy

Dear Mr. Malone:

There has been a change in our delivery service policy.

We have always provided free delivery for all orders regardless of size. Due to the increase in fuel prices, we must now limit this free delivery service to orders over $150. We regret the necessity of this change and hope it does not cause you any inconvenience.

We wish to take this opportunity to thank you for being one of our most valued customers.

Sincerely yours,

Temporary Price Decrease

Dear Mr. Domb:

This is my favorite kind of letter. Why, you ask, am I so happy? Read on.

This is to advise you that for a limited time, we are reducing prices on certain items in our catalog. Take a moment to look over the enclosed catalog. I have circled in red ink the items temporarily reduced. What an opportunity!

Please take advantage of these prices. If you wish to order

large quantities, or stagger shipments, give me a call and we can work out mutually acceptable terms and conditions.

Get your order in — these prices are only in effect until June 30.

I do enjoy writing this type of letter. Thank you in advance for your order.

Yours truly,

Moneyback Guarantee Policy

Dear Ms. Casuker:

I am delighted to announce that Scamm Books will offer a full moneyback guarantee on all book purchases starting today. This means that if you are not satisfied with any book purchased from us, simply return it for a full refund. You'll receive every penny back, no questions asked.

No other bookseller in the business offers you such an iron-clad guarantee. Maybe that's why Scamm Books is the largest bookseller on the East Coast.

We look forward to satisfying your book needs.

Sincerely,

Change of Service Representative

Dear Mr. Pansy:

Thank you for affording me the opportunity to meet with you and members of your staff.

I know Charles Wit serviced your account for years and made many friends. While his presence will be missed, I can promise you will continue to receive the fine service you have come to expect.

I am looking forward to visiting your plant again on Friday, April 4.

Cordially,

New Account Representative

Dear Mr. Dawn:

It is my great pleasure to inform you that Joyce Williams will now be representing our firm in your area.

Joyce has been handling our accounts in the Boston area for some time and is extremely knowledgeable in the field of health and fitness.

Your new representative is scheduled to visit your office on June 6.

Sincerely,

Appointment of New Representative

Dear Mr. Rollins:

We have assigned Walter Robin as our new representative for your area. Walter has been with our firm for some time and is extremely experienced in all aspects of our production.

Walter will be coming to Big Rapids on May 4 and will be calling on you in the morning if that doesn't conflict with your schedule. If there is any problem with that date, please let us know.

Cordially,

Notice of Rate Increase

Dear Mr. Heartless:

This letter confirms my telephone conversation with you today concerning an increase in our billing rate to $36 per hour. As discussed, it is necessary we request this increase due to a rise in the cost of conducting our business. We are faced with an increase in payroll taxes and insurance, along with an increase in our overhead costs.

Attached are copies of our service agreement. Please sign

one copy and return it to us indicating your approval of this new rate.

Sincerely,

Moving To A New Location

Dear Mr. Fergeson:

We are pleased to announce that we are moving to a larger, more modern building so we can better service your investment needs.

Starting June 1, our office will be located at 1631 Elm Street, Warren, Michigan.

Our new office is 5,200 square feet compared to our present 2,500. The building is fully air-conditioned and overlooks the Detroit River.

On behalf of the entire staff of Cheatum Investments, I want to thank you for the confidence you have shown in our company. Without your continuing support, our rapid growth would not have been possible.

You are personally invited to visit our new offices. During the entire month of June we will be serving complimentary beverages, sandwiches and snacks.

Sincerely yours,

Company Picnic

Dear Valued Staff:

Lincoln Tire and Rubber is pleased to announce that our annual summer picnic will be held Saturday, July 15, from noon until six o'clock at Soldier's Field Park. A detailed map is enclosed.

Every employee and all guests will receive one picnic lunch and refreshments. Enjoy all the refreshments you want, but please take only one lunch per person. After lunch, a number of competitive sporting events will be held, including baseball, volleyball and horseshoes. A drawing for a set of four Lincoln radial tires will be held at five o'clock.

Please let Marcia Fitty know whether you plan to attend and the number of guests you plan to bring. There is a limit of three guests per employee.

We are looking forward to seeing you.

Sincerely,

Sales Meeting

Dear Mr. Talbert:

I am pleased to announce that our first annual sales meeting will be held Friday, August 4, at eight o'clock at Kimberly Hall.

Mr. Bristol Foster has graciously offered to kick off the meeting with a talk on the psychology of closing the deal. It should be most inspiring since Bristol is a much sought after speaker.

I am looking forward to seeing you.

Sincerely,

Chapter 5

Letters of Complaint

Making a Complaint. When you are not satisfied with a product or service you should complain. Most successful companies welcome complaints because it provides valuable information on defective products, poor service or incompetent employees. Only when problems are brought to the attention of management can improvements be made. A complaint letter should provide all essential information about your dissatisfaction and specifically state what action or adjustment you expect. The tone of the letter should be reasonable and unemotional.

Answering a Complaint. No matter how efficient a company is, or how good its products or services are, customer complaints are inevitable. Generally complaints can be handled by following this proven formula:

1. Thank the customer for complaining and express regret about his dissatisfaction.

2. Explain in detail what you plan to do about the complaint.

3. Tell the customer why the problem occurred (if appropriate) and why it will not happen again.

4. Restate your appreciation to the customer for bringing the matter to your attention.

There will be times when the customer's complaint is unfounded or unreasonable. For example, when a customer requests a refund after using a product for several years while the guarantee period was only 30 days. When this happens, give convincing reasons for your position and offer some alternative, if available. Always close the letter on a friendly note.

Letter Accompanying Return of Product For Repairs

Gentlemen:

The watch I am returning was purchased on November 2, 1999 and is under warranty. The problem is the watch fails to keep accurate time. It gains approximately five minutes per hour.

Please make any adjustments necessary, and return the watch to the above address as soon as possible.

Sincerely yours,

Nonreceipt of Book

Gentlemen:

In my letter of June 3, I explained that the book I ordered had not arrived. I am attaching a copy of that correspondence for your convenience.

Having received neither the book, nor a response to my previous letter, I am requesting you refund the $16.95 remitted with my order. Attached is a copy of my cancelled check.

I shall be looking forward to receiving my refund promptly. Thank you for your immediate attention to this matter.

Yours cordially,

Written Confirmation of Verbal Complaint

Dear Mr. Carson:

This will confirm our telephone conversation today wherein I informed you there was a problem with the installation of the drinking fountain.

As I stated, the water pressure is too low, extending only about an inch above the spout.

It is my understanding you will repair the problem this Friday, March 4, at three o'clock.

Thank you for your cooperation in this matter.

Yours truly,

Letter Accompanying Return of Defective Product

Gentlemen:

The Vegematic I purchased on May 15 turned out to be a disappointment. While it looked the same as the one in your commercial, it did not perform the same way.

Following the instructions, I placed an onion in its proper position and pushed down on the mincer, which immediately bent out of shape. I experienced the same problem when I attempted to dice a carrot.

Therefore, I am returning the Vegematic and ask that you issue a full refund. I am not interested in receiving a replacement.

Yours truly,

Answering Complaint For Nonreceipt of Product

Dear Valued Customer:

Thank you for your letter of March 16 informing us that the book you ordered had not arrived.

We are sorry for the inconvenience this has caused and are sending another book to you today. In the event the original order is delivered to you, please call the toll-free number listed on our letterhead.

Please accept our apology and thanks for placing your order with us.

Cordially yours,

Acknowledging Report of Poor Service

Dear Mrs. Kalt:

Thank you for taking time to fill out our questionnaire during your stay at our hotel. We appreciate hearing from our customers, as their comments are vital for us to continue improving our accommodations and service.

The problems you mentioned have been brought to the attention of our housekeeping department. While the lack of service you experienced is unusual and not the standard of our hotel, there is no excuse for a lackadaisical attitude on the part of any of our employees. We are sorry for the inconvenience and annoyance this incident caused.

Thank you again for your comments. We hope you will give us another chance to serve you.

Yours truly,

Response to Product Complaint

Dear Mrs. Zitka:

We are sorry to hear you have been experiencing problems with your new Flash electric toothbrush.

While we do ask that our customers contact their dealer in the event of a problem, we recognize in your case that it would be impossible. Therefore, if you will carefully package the unit in its original carton and send it to us, our "doctors" will put it through a thorough examination to determine the problem.

If the problem turns out to be a minor adjustment, we shall make the repair and return the unit to you within thirty days. If we find the unit is defective, we will send you a replacement immediately.

Again, I am sorry you experienced this difficulty and wish to thank you for your patience.

Sincerely,

Reply to Product Complaint

Dear Valued Customer:

Your letter of April 14 has been received and we were very sorry to hear about the problem you experienced with our Jiffy Slicer.

We maintain rigid inspection standards, but occasionally an imperfection slips by, as it unfortunately did in your case.

We are shipping a replacement order to you at once. Your satisfaction is extremely important to us and we apologize for the inconvenience you have been caused.

Thank you for purchasing our products.

Sincerely,

Notice of Accounting Error

Gentlemen:

This is to acknowledge receipt of your invoice #611.

A check of our records indicates that payment for this invoice was made on April 4 with our check #1036, payable to you in the amount of $405.10.

Please review your records and bank deposits to be sure you have not received our payment. If you are still unable to find a record of payment, let me know and I will request a photocopy of our check and send it to your office. This normally takes about 30 days.

If I do not hear from you, I will assume you have found our payment and have appropriately credited our account.

Respectfully,

Request For Proof Merchandise Was Returned

Dear Mrs. Abdul:

In reference to your letter of June 1, we have no record of having received the merchandise you returned.

In order to issue a refund for the $10.95, we request you provide us with the following information:

1. Date you returned the merchandise.
2. Form of shipment (UPS, Post Office, etc.)
3. Copies of any correspondence to us in regard to returning merchandise.

Your cooperation in this matter will enable us to trace the parcel.

Thank you for your help. I will be looking forward to your letter.

Yours truly,

Adjustment For Shipping Excess Merchandise

Dear Mr. Betch:

Please accept our apology for having shipped merchandise in excess of the amount stated in your purchase order.

We have made an adjustment in your account to reflect this error and have arranged for pick up of the excess merchandise.

We are sorry for the inconvenience this has caused you and are most appreciative of your cooperation and understanding. Thank you.

Yours truly,

Returned Merchandise Received — Account Credited

Dear Mrs. Filli:

This is to acknowledge receipt of your letter of May 1, in which you requested a credit to your account for the merchandise damaged in transit.

Please be advised that your account has been credited in the amount of $151. We are sorry about the inconvenience this has caused you.

Thank you for your cooperation and understanding in this matter.

Sincerely yours,

Response to Damaged Goods Complaint

Dear Mr. Annoyince:

Your letter of May 14, in which you described the condition of the toaster you ordered, has been brought to my attention. We are very sorry this merchandise was damaged in transit.

Please return the damaged goods by placing the original carton inside a slightly larger box and attaching a copy of your letter on the outside of the package. Upon receipt of the merchandise, we will send you a replacement and a check to reimburse you for the extra shipping expense.

I am sorry for this inconvenience, but this procedure must be followed for insurance purposes.

Thank you for your understanding and patience.

Sincerely yours,

Letter Accompanying Refund Check

Dear Mrs. Fussy:

Having received the merchandise you returned, we are enclosing our check to you in the amount of $44.00.

Thank you for taking such care in packing the returned merchandise.

We are sorry circumstances prompted the return of this merchandise, but hope you will continue to allow us to serve you in the future.

Yours truly,

Second Request For Refund

Gentlemen:

On April 2, I attached my letter to the merchandise I returned to you and requested a refund. I have enclosed a copy of that letter for your convenience.

As you will note, quite some time has elapsed since I returned the merchadise and I have not yet received your check. I would appreciate it if you would take care of this matter as quickly as possible, since I am reluctant to order additional merchandise under the circumstances.

Thank you for your prompt attention to this matter.

Sincerely yours,

Warranty Expired — Must Charge For Repairs

Dear Mrs. Wilson:

We are sorry to hear of your problem with the Super Can-opener. We would like to be able to make the necessary adjustments at no charge to you, but unfortunately, the warranty has expired.

The proof-of-purchase you mailed to us indicates the product was purchased on November 2. Since our warranty is good for one year from date of purchase, it expired three months ago.

If you would like us to repair the Super Canopener, there will be a charge of $17.00. We guarantee the repairs for one year.

Please check the appropriate box on the enclosed instruction card and return it to us as soon as possible.

Sincerely yours,

Chapter 6

Credit

Most businesses could not survive without credit. It is virtually impossible for a company to do business without granting credit to its customers.

Since credit is so common in today's business world, few companies get upset about supplying credit information. Many problems can be avoided by establishing a firm credit policy that is applied consistently to all customers. People generally have no problem complying with an established company policy. It is only when someone feels singled-out that problems are likely to arise.

Request For Credit Information

Gentlemen:

It was with great pleasure that we received your recent order which was entered for immediate shipment.

To enable us to extend credit terms for future orders, please send us credit information. We have enclosed a simplified financial statement form for your convenience.

Thank you again for your order. We are looking forward to serving you in the future.

Sincerely yours,

Payment With Order Request — Credit Card Expired

Dear Mr. Wolet:

Thank you for your recent order for two Bomar Calculators.

We are unable to send you the products because your credit card has expired. If you still want your order, please send a check and we will be happy to send it immediately.

Thank you.

Sincerely,

Denial of Time Extension For Payment

Dear Mr. Bohind:

We regret to inform you we are unable to extend any more time for payment of the above invoice.

We feel we have been extremely patient and if we do not receive payment in full, on or before May 30, we will have no other choice but to turn this matter over to our attorney, with instructions to use all available legal remedies to collect the amount owed.

Cordially yours,

Request For Catalog and Credit Application

Gentlemen:

Our firm is interested in opening an account with your company. We carry an extensive line of computer hardware and software servicing the Central Florida area.

Would you please send us a current catalog price list and credit application.

I will be looking forward to receiving this material in the near future.

Sincerely,

Granting Extension of Time For Payment

Dear Mr. Hope:

Thank you for your letter of February 2 in which you explained the circumstances behind your request for an extension of time to remit your payment on invoice #126.

We do appreciate your straightforwardness and have noted on your account that your payment will be made on March 20.

You have been a loyal customer for some time and if this gesture on our part helps to ease your current situation, we are pleased to be of assistance.

Yours truly,

Notice of Credit Approval

Dear Ms. Casey:

It is our pleasure to notify you that a charge account has been approved in your name. We welcome you as a new customer and hope you enjoy the convenience of your new charge account.

A credit limit in the amount of $3,500 has been established.

Along with your card, we are enclosing a pamphlet explaining our billing procedure, how to use your credit card and additional information you should find useful.

Thank you for choosing to shop at our store.

Very truly yours,

Approval of Credit

Dear Mr. Wiesend:

We have reviewed your application for credit, and it is our pleasure to inform you an account has been opened for your company.

Please feel free to use your account as often as you wish. A descriptive brochure is attached which outlines the terms and conditions applicable to this account.

Should your credit requirements change, or if you have any questions regarding your new account, call this office and ask to speak to one of our account representatives. When you call, please have your account number available so we can gain quick access to your file.

Sincerely,

Name Change on Credit Card Request

Dear Ms. Copiloni:

My charge account with your company is currently held in my maiden name. Since I have recently married, I would appreciate it if you would change the name and address on my account to the following:

Account Number:	167
Name:	Sally Smith
Address:	126 Elm Street
City, State, Zip:	Cass, MI 48180

Please send me a new charge card reflecting this name change. Upon receipt of the new card, I will destroy the old card.

Thank you for your prompt attention to this matter.

Very truly yours,

Request For Payment With Order

Dear Mr. Rossi:

A review of your loan account shows three checks were returned unpaid from your bank over the past six months.

While we regret having to take this action, we must insist future payments on your loan be made by a certified check. Any payment not certified will be returned to you, possibly causing you to incur a late charge.

In making future payments, please send them to the attention of Mr. Adams for proper credit.

Your cooperation is appreciated.

Sincerely yours,

Denial of Credit

Dear Ms. Williams:

Thank you for your recent application for credit with our firm. I regret to inform you we cannot extend credit terms to you at this time based on the report we received from our credit bureau, TFT Associates.

If you feel there may be errors in the records of the credit reporting agency, we suggest you contact them and review their current information. In the event there have been errors made, please direct them to submit a revised report to us for reconsideration.

Meanwhile, we would be happy to welcome you as a customer. We have a layaway plan and various other options available to our cash customers.

Please feel free to call me if you have any questions or if I can be of assistance to you in any way.

Sincerely yours,

Notice of Increase In Credit Line

Dear Mr. Cassidy:

After reviewing your charge account, it pleases us to inform you we have increased your credit limit as follows:

> Old Credit Limit: $1,500
>
> New Credit Limit: $2,500

Furthermore, this change in account status qualifies you to use our installment account whereby purchases are not posted for 30 days after sale.

You will also be notified of our special customer sales we have from time to time. We appreciate your continued patronage and look forward to assisting you in the near future.

Yours truly,

Notice of Change In Credit Status

Dear Mr. Jackaloni:

You are one of our most valued accounts and it is with deep regret that I must advise you of a change in your account status.

From now on, it will be necessary that a check accompany each order for merchandise from your firm. We must insist upon this until your account is brought up to date, at which time we will reevaluate your open account status.

I know this will represent an inconvenience to you and I hope it will not interfere with our long and profitable relationship.

We value your business and look forward to resolving this difficulty in the immediate future. If I may be of assistance, please call me at your convenience.

Sincerely yours,

Letter Accompanying Late Payment

Dear Mr. Salvitino:

Enclosed is our payment in the amount of $621.50 which

should clear the balance in our account with you.

We are very sorry it has taken such a long time to remit our payment, but hope you will understand that we have been experiencing some serious cash flow problems. We are happy to inform you we are now on the road to recovery and expect a good year.

Thank you for the understanding and courtesy you have shown our company during this rough period.

Sincerely yours,

Extension of Payment Date

Dear Mr. Hardline:

My next installment payment will be due on May 1.

Due to an unexpected emergency, I will be unable to make this payment by the due date. Therefore, I am requesting an extension of 20 days to make this payment.

If you review my file, you will find previous payments have been made in a timely fashion. My relationship with your bank is important to me, as well as my desire to maintain a good credit rating.

Thank you very much for your consideration of this request.

Yours truly,

Refusing Request For Special Billing

Dear Mr. Sole:

Your letter, requesting we bill you quarterly rather than monthly, presents a problem.

We would like to welcome you as a new customer and accommodate you in any way possible. Your request, however, would result in receiving preferential treatment and would be unfair to our customers who must settle their accounts within 30 days. If we offered the terms you requested to all of our customers, we would soon be out of business.

I am sure you can understand our position in this matter. We welcome your business on our regular open account basis and hope we will have the opportunity to serve you.

Sincerely yours,

Chapter 7

Customer Correspondence

Most written correspondence generated by business is addressed to customers. Despite this, most businesses do not fully cultivate customer loyalty by use of written correspondence. For example, too few businesses send out thank you letters to customers who regularly place large orders, customers who always pay promptly, or customers who refer new customers. These letters don't have to be written, yet build good customer relations and loyalty.

No matter how hard a business strives, there will always be foul-ups: delays in shipments, the wrong merchandise sent and invoice errors. All these problems generally call for a written letter to the customer.

Thank You For Business — Restaurant

Dear Mrs. Willis:

It was our pleasure to serve you and your guests for the luncheon you held at our restaurant on Friday.

We hope our cuisine and service was satisfactory and you were pleased with having selected The Fish House for this event. We are always anxious to improve our high standards and would appreciate your comments or suggestions about the service we provided.

Thank you for giving us the opportunity to serve you.

Yours truly,

Thank You For Business — Travel Agency

Dear Mr. Rich:

Thank you for giving Travel-R-Us the opportunity to make your travel arrangements for your recent trip to Mexico City.

We hope you were pleased with the air travel and hotel accommodations we arranged for you. We encourage your comments. That's the best way for us to better serve you in the future.

We hope you will give us the opportunity to help plan your next vacation or business trip.

Thank you.

Cordially,

Acknowledgment Of Positive Employee Comments

Dear Mrs. Dimwat:

Thank you for your letter highlighting the exceptional treatment you received from one of our employees. A copy of your letter has been forwarded to the personnel department and will be included in the employee's file.

So seldom does a customer take time to write a letter of appreciation that I feel moved to reward your effort.

Please accept the enclosed certificate which will entitle the bearer to a ten percent discount on the merchandise being purchased at that time.

Again, on behalf of our entire organization, a heartfelt thank you.

Cordially,

Demand To Return Goods

Dear Mr. Janeway:

Certain goods have been shipped to you within the past ten

days as shown by the attached invoice.

It has come to our attention that your firm is insolvent and therefore we demand the return and reclamation of all goods delivered to you within the ten days preceding this notice.

If you have any questions, call me at 800-600-0000.

Very truly yours,

Notice of Shipment and Backorder

Dear Valued Customer:

Thank you for your order.

We have sent all the items you requested, except for item #621 which is backordered. That item will be shipped in four days.

We apologize for the delay and thank you for your patience.

Sincerely,

Response To Praise Of Product

Dear Mrs. Bullset:

I just received your letter regarding your Chambers Mixmaster and I would like to thank you for your kind words about our products. It is heartwarming to know this appliance remained with your family for nearly thirty years and never "let you down."

We updated our Chambers Mixmaster only once, and that occurred in the new 1976 models. Therefore, the model you are referring to would have to be our original style, model #3309. I regret to say we do not have any of the discontinued models. I can, however, assure you our current model, which is available in most department stores and appliance centers, has been made with the same fine quality. You may be surprised to know it comes with the same guarantee of workmanship and high quality we have been providing since 1946, the year when Chambers Appliances started in business.

I wish I could be of more help to you. Thank you again for the lovely letter you have written us.

Sincerely yours,

Notice Of Part Now In Stock

Dear Valued Customer:

We are happy to inform you the parts you ordered are now in stock and available for pickup at the above address.

Please accept our sincerest apologies for the delay in delivery. Thank you for your patience. As always, it is our intent to provide dependable and quality service and we appreciate your understanding in waiting.

If we may be of further assistance, please call any time.

Sincerely,

Appreciation of Product Comments

Dear Mr. Carter:

Thank you for the favorable review you gave our new product, the Stomach Flattner.

We are pleased that you found our product useful and reasonably priced.

We certainly enjoyed reading your review and would like to thank you once again for your kind words.

Sincerely,

Notice of Completed Repairs

Dear Mrs. Kanter:

As of this date, we have been unsuccessful in our attempts

to contact you. Your radio has been repaired and is ready for pick-up.

Since we will be closed from December 24 to January 2, we wanted to be sure you were given the opportunity to pickup your radio before we close for the holidays.

Please advise us of your intentions as soon as possible.

Sincerely yours,

Notice of Service Contract Expiration

Dear Mr. Tomes:

Your on-site Service Agreement has expired. We have not received a remittance or reply to our previous request for payment. Perhaps this was an oversight on your part, or perhaps your payment is in the mail.

If you do not send your payment within ten days, we will assume you do not wish to continue your Service Agreement.

Should you decide to terminate your Service Agreement, we will look forward to furnishing the same high quality service on your equipment at our hourly rate of $120 per hour, plus parts and travel expenses.

If payment has been made or if there are any questions regarding your account, please call.

Very truly yours,

Nobody Home For Repairman Visit

Dear Mrs. Raily:

On Friday, April 1, our serviceman came to your home to install your new dishwasher and found no one there. This was the date we had arranged for installation, but I know things like this can happen.

I would appreciate it if you will call me so we can arrange a convenient time to have this work done for you.

Sincerely,

Delayed Shipment Notice

Dear Mr. Flak:

This is to inform you we are unable to make delivery on the above referenced purchase order on the date indicated.

The merchandise should be ready to ship within 10 days of the original delivery date and we hope you can hold out until that time.

We did want to inform you of this delay promptly to give you as much time as possible to make alternative arrangements, if necessary. We assure you we will expedite delivery as soon as we receive the merchandise.

Please accept our apology for this delay and thank you for your understanding.

Sincerely,

Returned Merchandise Received — Account Credited

Dear Mr. Raymond:

We received the merchandise you returned and are pleased to advise you we have credited your account in the amount of $1,100. If you prefer, we will mail you a check for the full amount of the credit.

Please advise.

Yours truly,

Notice of Discount For Prompt Payment

Dear Mr. Villeman:

In the past twelve months, you have purchased a considerable amount of merchandise from us for which we are most appreciative.

Since you have never taken advantage of the 2% discount we offer for early payment, we thought you might be unaware of just how substantial your savings could be. The savings on last year's purchases alone would have amounted to $1,751.

By paying within 10 days of delivery, you can actually save 24% of the face amount of your average monthly bill over the period of a year. There are firms who prefer to borrow funds to take advantage of this discount. Of course, you know what is best for your business, but we want to be sure you are aware of this savings factor.

We would like to take this opportunity to thank you for the orders given us over this past year and the promptness of your payments. It is a pleasure doing business with your firm.

Very truly yours,

Discovery of Duplicate Payment

Dear Mrs. Olly:

Enclosed is our check for $46.00, representing a refund for your duplicate payment on invoice #630.

We are pleased our bookkeeping department discovered this overpayment so quickly.

Thank you.

Sincerely,

Response To Request For Distributor Information

Dear Mr. Comacozi:

Thank you for your recent inquiry regarding where our products can be purchased in your country.

We have not yet established foreign distribution for our products, and therefore they can only be purchased from one of our distributors in the United States. If you are interested in placing an order for any of our products, please direct your correspondence to:

Acme Sales
14 Elm Street
Wild Rapids, MI 46105

We have forwarded a copy of your letter to our distributor to acquaint him with your needs, should you decide to place an order.

Thank you so much for your interest in our products. If we can be of further assistance, please call any time.

Sincerely,

Response to Request For Wholesale Products

Dear Mr. Bolsome:

Thank you for your offer to represent our products.

While we wish we could accommodate your request, it has been a long standing policy of this company to sell direct and not through wholesalers.

We certainly appreciate the interest you have shown in our products and wish you well in your other endeavors. We will keep your name on file and notify you should our policy change.

Again, thank you for your kind thoughts of our company.

Yours truly,

Chapter 8

Collection Letters

The purpose of collection letters is to collect money owed you without losing the customer. Collection letters are usually written in a series, each successive letter stronger in tone than the previous one. Beginning letters are friendly — even humorous — but after about six or eight letters, there is an announcement that the matter is being referred to a collection agency or attorney. Since the objective is to collect, each letter must offer a chance to pay. Beginning letters demand immediate payment of the full amount owed while succeeding letters may offer more time to pay or even propose an installment payment plan.

Both federal and state laws regulate collection practices. Therefore, before establishing a collection policy, you should be aware of applicable laws governing harassment and privacy.

Explanation of Bounced Check

Dear Mr. Redding:

When I received your letter today with my check attached marked "insufficient funds," I called my bank immediately.

The Operations Manager at the bank, Joan Wilks, discovered the bank failed to credit my account with a substantial deposit made several days before.

The bank assured me they will send you a formal letter of apology for their error. Attached is my check in the amount of $120 to replace the dishonored check.

Sincerely yours,

Apology For Collection Letter Sent Erroneously

Dear Mr. Adams:

Thank you for your letter and photostat of your check showing your account had been paid in full. We are very sorry for the inconvenience this has caused you. Your cancelled check enabled us to pinpoint how this error occurred. Thank you for sending it.

Please accept our apology for the letter we wrote under the assumption this bill had not been paid. I know this must have been extremely frustrating for you, especially when you have always paid your bills promptly.

Thank you for your patience and please be assured we will do everything possible to ensure this type of error does not occur in the future.

Yours truly,

Notice of Bounced Check

Dear Mrs. Zola:

Your check made payable to Solar Products in the amount of $151.00 has been returned to us because of insufficient funds. The bank will not allow us to redeposit the check since it has already been presented on two occasions.

Would you please send the amount of the check, plus the $10.00 fee for our service charge for returned checks, to our office.

We must ask that this amount of $161.00 be paid by either certified check or money order.

If you have any questions, contact me at the above telephone number.

Thank you.

Yours truly,

Bad Check Notice

Dear Mr. James:

Your check in the amount of $33.99, tendered to us on February 3, 1999 has been dishonored by your bank.

Unless we receive good funds for said amount within 10 days of receipt of this notice, we shall have no alternative but to commence appropriate legal action for its recovery.

Very truly,

Final Notice Before Legal Action On Bad Check

Dear Ms. Riley:

We have repeatedly requested payment of $33.95 on your overdue account. Our demands for payment have been ignored.

Accordingly, we shall turn this account over for collection within the next ten days unless payment or an acceptable proposal for payment is obtained.

Enforced collection on this obligation may result in additional legal or court costs to you and may impair your credit rating.

Very truly yours,

Confirmation of Conversation Regarding Past Due Account

Dear Mr. Dondilli:

This is to confirm our recent telephone conversation regarding the past due balance of your account.

As I mentioned in our conversation, the current balance on the account is $110.25, of which $35 is now past due. We look forward to receiving your check within the next week to clear the past due charges on your account.

81

Once these charges have been cleared, we will be in a position to review the current credit arrangements for your account. Presently, all orders are being referred to us. Your check for the past due balance must be received before future shipments on credit can be made.

Your cooperation and prompt attention to this matter will be greatly appreciated. If you have any questions regarding your account, please contact me.

Sincerely,

Denial of Time Extension For Loan Payment

Dear Mrs. Simpson:

This is to acknowledge receipt of your letter today in which you requested a three-month extension on your installment loan.

After careful review, we regret to inform you we are unable to grant any further extensions for payment on your loan.

We are sorry about the difficulties you are experiencing, but we must insist on receiving your payment by October 15.

We hope you will be able to find another solution to your problem.

Yours truly,

Delinquent Payment Notice

Dear Mrs. Procrass:

The payment due us on July 1 in the amount of $151.00 has not been received.

Please give this matter your immediate attention and mail a check without further delay.

Very truly yours,

Notice of Overdue Account Balance

Dear Mr. Watkins:

Our records indicate that payment on your account is overdue in the amount of $36.50. If the amount has already been paid, please disregard this notice. If you have not yet mailed your payment, why not make out your check and place it in the enclosed envelope while this reminder has your full attention.

Thank you in advance for your cooperation in this matter.

Sincerely,

Request For Explanation For Non-Payment

Dear Mr. Darcy:

We feel there must be a reason why you haven't answered any of our inquiries about your overdue account in the amount of $136.

If there is a problem regarding the enclosed bill, won't you please telephone me at the above number so that we can discuss the situation. Whatever the source of the problem, we are in the dark about your situation until we hear from you.

If this has been an oversight, please use the enclosed envelope to mail us a check for the full amount today.

Thank you for your cooperation in the prompt handling of this matter.

Sincerely,

Request For Payment

Dear Ms. Stella:

Would you believe we simply detest writing letters such as this one? We know you certainly can't enjoy hearing from us under these circumstances.

I am referring to the fact your account has fallen far behind.

We want you to remain a customer of ours.

What do you say? Can we hear from you today? We even placed a stamp on the enclosed envelope for your remittance.

If you are unable to send us the payment, please give me a call at the above telephone number.

Thank you.

Sincerely,

Request For Payment and Status of Credit Card

Dear Mrs. Stanford:

We are writing this letter to you because we do not want you to experience unnecessary embarrassment.

Your account is past due and I am sorry to inform you that if you were to present your charge card at our store today, our sales personnel could not accept the charge without an okay from the credit department. This would necessitate your going to the credit department to discuss the status of your bill before the charge would be approved.

You have been too good a customer to have to go through this procedure. But unless we receive your payment, we have no other alternative.

We have enclosed a self-addressed envelope for your convenience and are requesting that you please mail us your payment today. Thank you for your cooperation.

Sincerely,

Request For Payment — Good Businessman Appeal

Dear Mr. Frances:

As a good businessman, you are aware how accounts that

have become seriously past due must be handled. I am not going to use some clever phrase or witty jingle to get your attention. Neither do I wish to embarrass, intimidate or do any of the nasty things that are often done to encourage payment.

I am merely informing you the account has reached a point where we must decide within a few days whether to turn it over for collection or just hand it to our attorneys, neither of which is our preference.

We know you understand our predicament and are probably experiencing a similar situation with some of your accounts.

We would like to hear from you and learn what your intentions are regarding this account.

Thank you.

Sincerely,

Payment Plan Proposal

Dear Mr. Alexander:

This is to inform you that I am in receipt of your letter of March 1 and I acknowledge my account is in arrears in the amount of $736.40

We have been experiencing some difficulties lately in collecting our accounts receivable and unfortunately the domino theory has become a reality.

In fairness to all of our creditors, I would like to suggest that I send you $73.64 per month for a period of 10 months in order to satisfy this obligation. I am enclosing the first check for $73.64 as a sign of good faith and hope this proposal will be acceptable to you. It is understood, should we be successful in our attempts to collect some of our larger receivables during the next few months, I will be happy to remit the entire balance owing on this account.

Please let me hear from you regarding the proposal I have

outlined. Thank you for your patience and understanding in this regretable situation.

Sincerely,

Notice To Stop Sending Collection Letters

Gentlemen:

This is the third letter I have written regarding the status of my account.

I am enclosing copies of my previous letters to avoid going over the same information.

I am beginning to get annoyed by all the nasty notices you have been sending me *in error* and would appreciate someone straightening out the problem.

I understand the difficulty you must have in maintaining all of your records. But I am insisting my correspondence be read and that notices stop until this problem is resolved.

Thank you.

Sincerely,

Second Request For Payment

Dear Mr. Robinson:

By letter dated May 1, 1999, we informed you that $416.00 remained overdue on your account. To date, no payment from you has been received. We once again request payment.

Very truly yours,

Demand For Immediate Payment

Dear Mr. Kurtus:

We have contacted you several times by letter and phone

about payment of your account.

The following items are still overdue:

No. 162	March 6, 1999	$124.10
No. 171	April 4, 1999	$ 69.40
No. 194	May 15, 1999	$106.20

So far we have not received any sign of your cooperation. Therefore, we must insist on immediate payment. Please use the enclosed envelope to send your payment now.

Sincerely,

Installment Agreement

Dear Mrs. Chuckle:

This letter serves to confirm our agreement of April 5, 1999, in which you acknowledge the outstanding overdue debt of $610.50 to our company. We agreed that you shall make consecutive monthly payments of $61.50 until the debt is satisfied in full. We further agreed that I would receive the first payment by April 30, 1999 and each successive payment every month thereafter.

I sincerely appreciate your cooperation in resolving this matter. Finally, would you acknowledge our agreement by signing the enclosed copy of this letter and returning it to me in the enclosed, self-addressed envelope.

Very truly yours,

Final Notice Before Legal Action

Date:

Re: $94.40 Past Due

Dear Mrs. Wallace:

We have repeatedly requested payment of the above past due account. Our demands for payment have not been answered.

Therefore, we shall turn this account over for collection within the next 10 days unless payment or an acceptable proposal for payment is received.

Collection action on this obligation may result in additional legal or court costs to you and may impair your credit rating.

Very truly yours,

Chapter 9

Employee Communications

There are many types of employee communications — from a letter setting up a job interview to a letter terminating employment.

It is a good idea to inform employees of important policy decisions and orders in writing. This will help insure that these matters are followed and not forgotten.

Employee letters are an excellent way to build employee goodwill, morale and loyalty. Often a written expression of appreciation for a job well done is worth more than a pay raise. Many successful companies have a policy of writing a letter of appreciation whenever an employee does more than the job calls for.

Request For Job Interview

Dear Mr. Atkins:

Ruth Bessi recommended I contact you and request an interview.

I recently graduated from City College with a degree in business. I am very interested in the Denver area and would appreciate the opportunity to discuss any openings you may have.

I have enclosed my resume for your review and will look forward to meeting you.

Thank you for your consideration.

Sincerely,

Scheduling A Possible Employment Meeting

Dear Mr. Haroldson:

Thomas Stark has been with our firm for several years and has been one of our outstanding employees in the accounting department. For family reasons, he is moving to your area and we are truly sorry to lose him.

He has all the qualities you would expect from a good employee and I honestly feel any firm hiring him will be quite fortunate.

I believe it could be mutually beneficial if the two of you could meet once he arrives in Denver. He is mature and, of course, realizes there may not be an opening for him at this time.

Shall I suggest he make an appointment with you? I will be looking forward to your reply.

Cordially yours,

Job Interview Notice

Dear Mr. Taylor:

Thank you for your recent application for employment with The Chambers Corporation.

An interview has been scheduled for you on Monday, June 7, at 10:00 a.m., with Mr. Phil Menet, Head of Personnel. Mr. Menet's office is located on the 10th floor, room 1009, at the main office on Elm Street.

A test will be given immediately following your interview, which will take approximately one hour.

If you are unable to keep this appointment, or if you have any questions, please call me at (800) 555-4000.

Sincerely,

Thank You For Job Interview

Dear Mr. Clyde:

Thank you for the time and consideration extended me during my interview with you yesterday.

I appreciate the opportunity to speak with you about my experience and future goals.

I shall look forward to hearing from you and wish to thank you again for your courtesy.

Sincerely yours,

Thank You For New Uniforms

Dear Mr. Rainey:

All of the female flight attendants with Cambers International Airlines have asked that I write this letter to thank you for their new Bill Blass designed uniforms. We all agree this new design allows freer movement, is more comfortable and is absolutely "smashing." Therefore, on behalf of all of your flight attendants, thank you for having such good taste!

Very truly yours,

Recommendation Letter

To whom it may concern:

This will confirm that Jonathan Deering has been employed by Electro Flo for approximately four years. During his tenure of employment, he has displayed a unique ability to identify and solve problems. He has been instrumental in streamlining our accounting department. His experience in the accounting and finance area has been a valuable asset, one which can be of great value to any company using his services. He is loyal and always places the welfare of the company above all else. His patience with employees and his ability to communicate with management make him an ideal employee. If available, he can certainly count on re-employment with our firm, should the opportunity arise.

Any company considering Jonathan for employment has my most enthusiastic recommendation. If his performance here is any indication, he is destined to achieve new heights in his career.

Sincerely,

Notice of Bonus

Dear Stuart:

Please accept the enclosed Christmas Bonus with our very best wishes for a happy holiday season.

We wish to thank you for your role in making 1999 the most successful year in the history of our firm and we are all looking forward to a prosperous New Year.

To your wife and family, we extend our very best wishes for a Merry Christmas and a happy New Year.

Sincerely yours,

Positive Information on Past Employee

Dear Mr. Jenson:

This is to acknowledge receipt of your inquiry of March 5, in which you requested information on a previous employee of our firm.

Joyce Watson was my personal secretary for the last three years. She is intelligent, dependable and extremely well organized. She is fastidious in her appearance and is very conscientious about her work.

I have no hesitation in recommending her.

Sincerely,

Denial For Information on Past Employee

Dear Mr. George:

It is against the policy of our company to release any detailed information on the performance of our previous employees. Our records show that Cynthia Wills was employed by us from January 7th, 1995 to March 30, 1999. We are sorry we cannot be of further assistance.

Sincerely,

Denial of Letter of Recommendation

Dear Mr. Dale:

Your request for a letter of recommendation from our firm cannot be granted. While the work you performed was satisfactory, we do not feel it would be fair to either you or our firm to evaluate your capabilities based on a two month tenure of employment.

If any inquiries are made of us, we will reply most favorably. We wish you the best of luck in the future.

Sincerely yours,

Notice to Renew Drivers License

Dear Sabrina:

Our records indicate your driver's license needs to be renewed on or before March 6.

As you know, it is essential all employees who drive company vehicles keep their licenses current. We wanted to advise you of this now to provide ample time to renew your license.

Sincerely,

93

Letter Admonishing Employee

Dear Paula:

Henry Wimp, one of our customers, called my office today to inform me that he had been treated in an extremely discourteous manner by you.

He was referring to a telephone call on March 6 wherein he claims you stated you were too busy to find the answer to his question and you seemed totally indifferent to his problem.

If his complaint is valid, this kind of behavior is, of course, completely against our policy which is to make every attempt to help customers with problems. Without customers, we have no company.

I would like you to find the source of Mr. Wimp's problem and attempt to solve it with an apology, if warranted. Then report back to me on the result of your efforts.

Sincerely,

Request For Character Reference

Dear Mr. Craine:

Michael Ray has applied with our company for a position in our bookkeeping department. He has given your name as a character reference. Would you be kind enough to provide us with your written evaluation of this individual? Please be assured your response will be treated with confidentiality. Thank you.

Sincerely,

Request For Employment Reference

Dear Mr. Small:

We have received an application of employment from Amos Ally seeking a position with our firm in the capacity of janitor. We understand the applicant was previously employed by your firm.

Accordingly, we would appreciate a reference on this individual, including confirmation of the dates of employment, performance evaluation and reasons for termination.

Thank you for your cooperation.

Very truly yours,

Thank You For Job Application

Dear Ms. Hussy:

Thank you for your recent application for employment with Bolor Ball Bearings.

We regret to inform you there are no openings at this time. While we know this is disappointing news, we would like to retain your application in our files for future openings.

Thank you for your interest in working for our company.

Sincerely,

Thank You For Job Application

Dear Mrs. Wiloso:

Thank you for your recent application to join our company as a sales representative.

While we do not have an opening in your area at this time, we will certainly keep your application on file. Should a position become available, we shall inform you and arrange a convenient time for testing.

Cordially yours,

Job Interview Follow-Up Letter

Dear Mr. Lamoro:

It was a pleasure meeting with you yesterday and having

the opportunity to discuss your education and career goals.

I appreciate your candidness and feel that since your objectives are to work in the field of biogenics, you should attempt to obtain a position with a firm that would enable you to gain experience in this area. Unfortunately, our business does not afford you this opportunity.

I am certain you will find a position which suits you since you have a great deal to contribute.

Please accept my best wishes for your future.

Sincerely yours,

Notice of Employee Vacation Policy

Dear Staff Members:

This is to provide notice to all employees of our new company policy regarding vacations.

Notice of your intention to take a vacation must be given no less than 30 days prior to the start of your vacation. This will enable us to employ temporary help, if necessary, and to schedule vacations in a manner that will not be disruptive to operations.

Thank you for your cooperation.

Sincerely,

Employee Ineligible For Bonus

Dear Willie:

Each employee who has been with our firm for six months or more receives a Christmas bonus. Since you became a member of our sales department on August 1st, you will not be receiving a bonus this year.

I wanted to be sure that you understood this policy prior to disbursement of holiday paychecks to avoid any misunderstanding or disappointment on your part.

We are very pleased with your work and while we would like to bend the rules, this would be unfair to all of our other personnel.

Cordially yours,

Elimination of Bonus

Dear Mr. Paulson:

This has been a difficult year for the Chambers Corporation. I am sure you know the loss of three contracts with the United States Air Force, due to the cut-back in defense appropriations, hurt us substantially.

In July, we had a major decision to make. The question facing us was whether to let some of our employees go, or to explore other avenues of cost reduction, keeping everyone's job intact. We chose the latter course. Unfortunately, one of the benefits we were forced to eliminate this year was our annual Christmas bonus.

This will be the first year since 1976 that we will be unable to thank you in this special manner for your hard work, loyalty and faithfulness. We are hoping 1999 will be a prosperous year and that we will be able to reinstate our traditional Christmas bonus policy.

Best regards,

Exit Letter to Employee

Dear Marie:

Your decision to leave the firm has just been brought to my attention. We are very sorry to lose you inasmuch as your work has always been most satisfactory and we were hoping you would remain with the company for many years. I understand you are leaving for personal reasons having nothing to do with the organization.

I will be happy to provide you with a letter of recommendation, if you so request. You may find this helpful in securing a position with another firm in your new locale. Please advise my secretary of your intent in this matter so we can have it prepared for you before your departure.

I know that I speak for everyone at the company in wishing you the very best of luck in the future.

Sincerely,

Denial of Request For Raise

Dear John:

This is to acknowledge your letter of December 4. You are definitely to be commended for your progress with our company during the past two months.

I do believe, however, your request for a raise is premature. I feel it would be more appropriate to discuss a salary increase after you have worked here six months. If you continue on the same path, I am certain your request will be given careful consideration.

You are doing a fine job, keep up the good work!

Sincerely,

Letter of Praise For Employees

Dear Staff:

Our "Talent Night" promotion was greeted with a great deal of enthusiasm by the community and I want to take this opportunity to thank you for all of your support and hard work.

While the entire staff should be commended, I must single out one individual who worked exceptionally hard to make it such a success. This is Judith Blakely, who seems to have an unlimited amount of energy and holds firmly to the conviction that if it is worth doing, it is worth doing right! It is fair to say that without her help, this event would not have been nearly as successful as it was. We played to a full house. What more is there to say!

We will be looking forward to a repeat performance. It has been a joy working with you all.

Thanks again.

Cordially yours,

Letter of Praise To Employee

Dear Terry:

You are to be highly commended for the way you handled the emergency that occurred yesterday. Your efficient administering of CPR was an inspiration to all who watched in amazement while you revived that elderly woman who apparently stopped breathing.

The paramedics informed me that if you hadn't acted as quickly as you did, our customer's attack might have been fatal. Thanks to you, she is already out of intensive care and on the road to recovery.

We are very proud to have you in our organization.

Yours truly,

Letter of Praise To Employee

Dear Sally:

The displays you created for the "Summer's Coming" promotion are just beautiful. Several of the sales personnel told me they have received numerous compliments from customers.

Congratulations on a job well done.

Sincerely,

Employee Recognition on Anniversary

Dear Barbara,

Today marks your fifth anniversary as an employee of Parker Products. I would like to take this opportunity to thank you for those past five years of fine work and company loyalty.

I know the growth and success of our company is dependent on having strong and capable staff members such as yourself.

I hope you will remain with us for many years to come and I would like to offer my congratulations on this anniversary.

Cordially yours,

Invitation to Retirement Party

Dear Staff:

You are cordially invited to attend a party given in honor of James Brown on his retirement from Spartan Motorcar Company.

The party will be held at Cobo Hall on Friday, June 4, at seven o'clock. The company will be presenting James with a gift at that time.

Be prepared to eat, drink, dance and share in this farewell to James.

Cordially yours,

Congratulations On Promotion

Dear Mary:

Congratulations on your recent promotion to Operations Manager.

I know how hard you have worked to earn the recognition you enjoy at Kelly's, and I feel they are very wise in making the choice they did.

Please accept my best wishes for success in your new position.

Yours cordially,

Follow-Up To Job Test

Dear Mr. Wilson:

Thank you for taking the time to be tested for employment at our main office yesterday. We are giving your application our fullest consideration.

Within two weeks we should be able to provide you with a decision on your application. If, for some reason, we are uanble to offer you a position, we will have your application and aptitude test on record which will enable us to contact you when there is an opening.

We would like to thank you again for your time and interest in our company.

Sincerely,

Confirmation of Job Offer

Dear Mr. Carlson:

We are pleased to confirm your being employed by our firm in the capacity of file clerk. You will report directly to 543 State Street, Detroit, MI 48180, commencing with the start of employment on May 1, 1999 at eight o'clock.

Your salary shall be $9.00 per hour. You will also be covered by the standard group benefit plans and fringe benefits explained to you. For the first year, vacation time shall be pro-rated, so you will be entitled to 10 days vacation for this year.

If you agree this letter sets forth our understanding, please sign the enclosed copy and return for our files.

We look forward to your joining the company.

Very truly yours,

Notice of Promotion

Dear Mr. Harrison:

It is our great pleasure to inform you that you have been promoted to the position of Chief Accountant.

This promotion is in recognition of the fine work you have done for this firm. We are confident you will meet the new responsiblities of this position with the same level of enthusiasm and enterprise you have exhibited since you came to work for us.

Please accept our congratulations on your promotion.

Sincerely,

Acknowledgement of Application

Dear Mr. Harvey:

We appreciate your interest in being employed by our firm.

We regret to inform you, however, that the available position has been filled and we cannot give your application further consideration at the present time.

Your application will be kept on file for future reference should an opening arise.

Very truly yours,

Request For Employment Reference

Dear Mr. James:

Your former employee, Ralph Burger, has applied to our firm for employment as a salesperson.

We are writing to request information concerning Mr.

Burger's (1) dates of employment; (2) rate of compensation; (3) performance evaluation; and (4) reason for termination of employment.

Would you also please state whether he would be eligible for re-employment with your firm.

Any information furnished by you will be held in strictest confidence.

Thank you for your kind attention and cooperation.

Very truly yours,

Employee Suspension Notice

Dear Mr. Ahole:

On February 6, 1999, you received written notice of certain performance deficiencies and a warning that unless your performance improved, further disciplinary action would be taken against you, including possible suspension. Since then, I have attempted to assist you by having several supervisors explain why coming in late disrupts operations. However, your performance continues to be unsatisfactory by continuing to be late for work.

Therefore, commencing April 6, 1999 and continuing through April 16, 1999, you are suspended from your duties, without compensation.

Any further disciplinary action taken against you may include the termination of your employment.

———————————————————————

I acknowledge receipt of this warning.

———————————————————————
Employee

Involuntary Discharge From Employment

Dear Mr. Tyson:

We regret to inform you that effective March 4, 1999, your employment with the company is terminated for the following reason: Punching a fellow employee causing serious facial injury.

As of said date, you are required to vacate the premises with whatever personal possessions you may have.

Very truly yours,

_____

I hereby acknowledge receipt.

_____
Employee

Letter of Resignation — No Specific Reason

Dear Mr. Borrelli:

It is with great sadness that I tender my resignation to you.

Although there is much to say, I believe the reasons leading to this decision are known by you, and I will therefore leave them unsaid at this time.

I appreciate the opportunity of being a member of World Savings for so many years and offer my best wishes for your continued success.

Cordially yours,

Letter of Resignation — Work In Home State

Dear Mr. Yakoma:

This is to inform you that an opportunity has presented

itself that will enable me to work in my home state of Michigan.

I am therefore tendering my resignation and wish to advise you that March 1 will be my last day of employment.

I would like to thank you for the opportunity to work for D-Best Co., a truly outstanding organization.

Cordially yours,

Request For Information On
Developing Letter Writing Standards

Dear Mr. Lake:

The company is launching an extensive program to improve its written communications. The objectives of this program are to reduce communication costs, standardize communication practices and forms, and develop a company communications manual.

Mr. Milton Powell has asked me to write to the General Managers and obtain the following information to assist in meeting these goals:

- Your opinion on establishing standard procedures for writing letters, reports, and inter-office memorandums.

- Carbon copies of all correspondence sent from your plant for the week of October 15, 1999.

- Your suggestions as to how we can cut costs and increase the effectiveness of company communications.

The success of this program depends on the wholehearted cooperation of all employees. I will appreciate receiving this information by November 15, 1999.

Sincerely,

Request For Lecture By A Consultant

Dear Dr. Smith:

The Household Power Products Company of Chicago, Illinois is launching a program to improve its written communications. An important part of this program will be a one-day communications conference on November 7, 1999. Management personnel from all company plants will attend this conference at our Chicago office.

Mr. John Hopkins of the Investors Research Corporation of Chicago, Illinois has highly recommended you as an expert in the communications field. I have also been inpressed by your recent book, *Reply Please*, on communicating effectively.

We would like to retain you for a one-day lecture on November 7, 1999.

Our goals for this lecture period are as follows:

- Reduce communication costs.

- Standardize communication practices and forms.

- Effectively represent the company in correspondence with our customers.

Please advise whether or not you are interested in accepting this assignment. If you are, I will discuss this program with you in greater detail at your convenience. I can be reached from 8 a.m. to 5 p.m. at 501-2000.

An early reply will be appreciated.

Sincerely yours,

Planned Agenda During Visit

Dear Mr. Willis:

The first phase of the program to improve our written communications is now finalized. During your visit to the home office for the annual managers' conference, one day will be set aside for a talk by Dr. John C. Smith, noted author, lecturer and consultant on communications.

This talk on "The Principles of Business Reports and Letters" should be very informative and interesting and will greatly enhance our program of improving our communications.

A question and answer session will follow Dr. Smith's talk. Therefore, please be prepared to submit a list of questions that you consider pertinent to any communication problem that you have experienced.

I know from your previous letter that you are enthusiastic about this program and we can count on your support to meet the goals we have outlined.

Sincerely,

Open Letter To Employees On Written Communication

To: All Employees

Subject: Written Communications

During a recent conference, Dr. John C. Smith, noted author, lecturer and consultant on written communications, addressed a company management group and stressed the following ten principles important to effective communications:

1. Keep sentences short.

2. Write to express, not impress.

3. Prefer the simple to the complex.

4. Avoid unnecessary words.

5. Use active instead of passive voice.

6. Make full use of variety.

7. Consider the intelligence level of the reader.

8. Avoid dangling phrases and clauses.

9. Organize your communication.

10. Avoid improperly related pronouns.

All employees are urged to carefully read these ten principles and apply them to all written communications.

Your complete cooperation will result in an immediate overall improvement in the quality of company correspondence.

Sincerely,

Outline of Proposed Communications Manual

Dear Mr. Aly:

I have prepared a basic outline of information which I believe is important to include in the Communication Manual. I have listed these under the following two headings:

How to Think About Letters

- Plan your letter.

- Consider *who* is saying *what* to *whom* for what *effect.*

- Cover the subject completely, but be brief enough to be interesting.

- Use active rather than passive voice.

- Remember that your letters represent the company.

The Form of Our Company's Letters

- Use standard size 8½x11 white bond paper for the original copy.

- Use standard size 8½x11 vellum paper for all carbon copies.

- Use semi-block form.

I will discuss these recommendations in greater detail at your convenience.

Sincerely,

Request For Comments On Company Manual

Dear Mr. Blake:

If you recall, the personalizing of letters was discussed at great length with Dr. John Smith during the recent communications conference. His arguments for this format of writing were overwhelming. He also emphasized that many companies which are recognized as leaders in the field of communications use "personalized letters."

Beside his reputation as a noted author and lecturer, Dr. John Smith is a communications consultant for the most progressive companies in the country. Therefore, his opinions represent more than a "lot of nonsense."

In answer to your question, "Is it necessary that the forms and methods in the manual be followed?" I would like to point out that Mr. Norman C. Smith, President of Household Power Products, in an introductory statement in the manual, urged every employee to read it carefully and apply it in his day-to-day communications.

Your comments in regard to the manual are appreciated.

Sincerely,

Response To Comments On Company Manual

Dear Mr. Kep:

If you recall, your arguments that "we get into the twentieth century by using simplified letters without salutations, complimentary closes, etc." was thoroughly discussed with Dr.

John Smith during the question and answer session at the communications conference.

As he pointed out, your approach to writing communications may well be the writing format of the future, but is not now generally accepted as being in good taste. This opinion was agreed upon at the General Office during the many discussions we had on this subject.

We, of course, are disappointed in your reaction to the manual as expressed in your letter. I am certain if you apply these principles of written communications, you will be surprised at the gratifying results obtained.

I would like to suggest that you follow the recommendations of the manual for a thirty day period and then write me again. I am sure that you may then agree that our new approach to written communications has definitely improved company correspondence.

I would like to point out that Mr. Norman C. Wood, President of the Household Power Products Company, has completely endorsed the use of this manual.

Your comments in regard to the manual are welcomed and we will appreciate hearing from you again at your convenience.

Sincerely,

Suggestions For Improving Company Letters

Dear Mr. Walker:

I hope that your interest in our program for improving communications was a direct result of some recent company correspondence sent to you from our branch offices. We are proud of the improvement made in our written communications and hope that our customers are also benefitting.

Our program originated with a goal to reduce communication costs, standardize communication practices and forms, and a desire to effectively represent the company in correspondence with our customers.

I know we have met the first two goals and I hope your inquiry means we are meeting our third goal.

Based on my experience in developing and putting our program into effect, I would like to suggest that the most important criteria for the success of your program is to first sell your management on the need for improving communications and obtain their wholehearted support. Once you have this support, you can proceed with assurance that your program will be a success.

If you wish, I will forward a copy of a talk Dr. John C. Smith, noted author, lecturer and communication consultant gave to our management personnel. Much of his thinking on written communications was included in a communications manual which we have developed for all employees. I will also furnish a copy of this manual for your reference.

Please write and let me know if you can use this material and whether I can be of further assistance. I hope your program for improving communications is a complete success.

Sincerely,

Chapter 10

Supplier Communications

Suppliers provide most everything needed by a business from the merchandise sold to customers to everyday office supplies. As a result, a considerable amount of written correspondence is normally directed to suppliers.

A good deal of written correspondence with suppliers generally relates to placing orders or confirmations of verbal orders. Then, of course, you have correspondence relating to foul-ups: shipment of the wrong merchandise, incomplete orders, defective goods and invoice errors.

Letters to suppliers should normally be brief, to the point and businesslike.

Incomplete Shipment Notice

Gentlemen:

The shipment we received on the above referenced purchase order was incomplete. The following parts were missing:

One - XT 461

One - AT 522

We would appreciate it if you would rush the missing parts to us immediately. If you are unable to do so, please call me upon receipt of this letter.

Thank you for your prompt attention to this matter.

Yours truly,

Placing An Order

Gentlemen:

Please send me the following items from your spring catalog:

1	Owl 10″ Color TV	#AC1645	$299	(7.50)	$306.50
1	Dog Race Analyzer	#WNW209	$ 50	(3.50)	$ 53.50
				Total:	$360.00

I am enclosing my check in the amount of $372.25 which includes the cost of handling and shipping. Thank you.

Sincerely,

Error In Shipment Notice

Gentlemen:

This is to acknowledge receipt of the above referenced order and to inform you there is an error in the shipment.

The merchandise I ordered was brown color combs, while

the merchandise I received was black color combs.

Upon receiving your instructions for return of the goods, I will ship them to you at your expense.

I would like to receive the correct merchandise as quickly as possible and will appreciate your prompt attention to this matter.

Yours truly,

Notice of Receipt of Defective Goods

Gentlemen:

We are in receipt of merchandise shipped to us pursuant to your invoice number 1021, dated May 3, 1999.

Certain goods as listed on the attached sheet are defective for the following reasons:

Coats wrong style. Shipped style 14B. Should be 16A.

Accordingly, we reject said defective goods, demand credit or adjustment and intend to reship said goods to you at your expense.

Please confirm credit and issue instructions for return of defective goods.

Very truly yours,

Cancellation Notice

Gentlemen:

I am in receipt of your notice that there will be a two week delay in shipment of the above referenced merchandise.

This delay is unacceptable and we are therefore cancelling our purchase order number 612 for the above items.

Yours truly,

Cancellation Notice

Gentlemen:

Our customer has informed us she can wait no longer for the merchandise we ordered from you on February 1, 1999.

We are therefore cancelling our purchase order number 721 which was contingent on delivery prior to April 1.

Under the circumstances, we are certain you will understand the necessity of our cancelling this order.

Yours truly,

Decline To Distribute Product

Dear Mr. Balding:

Thank you for submitting your hair formula to us for review and evaluation.

Currently, we are distributing several products of a similar type and I don't feel it appropriate to make further additions at this time. Should our policies change in the future, we will consider your product as a candidate for distribution.

Should you develop or wish to submit other products in the future, please feel free to contact us. Again, thank you for considering us as a potential distributor.

Sincerely,

Decline to Distribute Product

Dear Mr. Bimbo:

Thank you for submitting your automatic fizzer to us for review and evaluation.

Based on results of our technical evaluation, our marketing review committee made the decision not to accept your product for distribution at this time. A copy of our Evaluation Summary Sheet is attached for your information.

Should you wish to submit other products in the future, please feel free to contact us. Again, thank you for considering us as a potential distributor.

Sincerely,

Request For Prices and Ordering Information

Gentlemen:

Your advertisement in the June issue of *Hardware News* is of great interest to us.

We would like to know more about the products your firm offers and would appreciate receiving your wholesale price list and information regarding terms and ordering.

It is our desire to offer our customers the widest selection possible and we are always interested in new products.

We look forward to your prompt response. Thank you.

Respectfully,

No Record of Purchase

Dear Mr. Perry:

After receiving your letter today, we conducted a thorough search through our files and found no record of our firm purchasing any merchandise from your company.

We would appreciate your sending us documentation supporting this claim.

Thank you for your cooperation and patience in this matter.

Sincerely,

Request For Insurance Premium Refund

Dear Mr. Lovelace:

Your letter dated April 15, 1999 stated I would be receiving a refund for the unused portion of prorated insurance coverage provided under the above referenced policy.

As of this date, I have not received this check. Since I have moved, I am concerned the check may have been sent to the wrong address.

Would you please let me know if a check has been mailed? If not, I would appreciate your authorizing one to be sent to the address above.

Thank you for your attention to this matter.

Sincerely yours,

Notice of Non-Conforming Goods

Dear Mr. Chin:

We have received certain goods from you under the attached invoice. Some of the goods received do not conform to our specifications because the rubber thickness is less than $\frac{1}{4}$ inch.

Therefore, we reject these goods and demand a credit or cash refund. We will reship to you at your expense.

Very truly yours,

Firm Offer To Sell

Dear Mr. Williams:

We hereby offer to sell to you a 1987 Spartan II Motorcar (Engine #463174125) for the price of $425.00 and agree that this offer will be held open for not more than 30 days.

Sincerely,

Stop Payment Order To Bank

Gentlemen:

You are hereby directed to stop payment upon presentation

of the following check:

Name of Payee:	Thomas Wolf
Date of Check:	November 5, 1999
Amount:	$346.51
Check Number:	1071

This stop payment order shall remain in effect until further written notice.

_____

Name of Account

_____

Account Number

By: _____

Chapter 11

Sales Letters

The sales letter is one of the most powerful sales tools available to a business. And it is one of the cheapest ways to solicit business, especially compared to a personal sales call.

In a broad way, virtually all letters are sales letters in the sense they strive to sell products, services, ideas, company image or your position on something. This section focuses primarily on sales letters that solicit business for products or services.

The First Sentence

The first sentence is the most important part of the sales letter. It must attract and hold the reader's attention. If it doesn't accomplish this, all is lost because no product or service will be sold.

There are certain types of opening sentences that are proven to get and hold the reader's attention. These types of sentences include the following:

- **Sentences that promise a free gift:**
  "I've enclosed a free sample import so you can see for yourself the beauty of these products."

- **Sentences that offer something new and different:**
  "Announcing the first computer the size of a postage stamp."

- **Sentences that ask a question:**
  "Would you like to buy a new Spartan Motorcar for nothing down?"

- **Sentences that make a challenge:**
  "I defy you to find a lower price for a Swiss-made watch!"

How the Reader Perceives Value

One of the most important formulas for writers of sales letters to understand is:

$$VALUE = \frac{BENEFITS}{PRICE}$$

When a potential customer reads your letter, he subconsciously uses this formula to decide whether or not to buy your product or service.

The reader wants to know what he will gain — what benefit he will get —compared to how much money must be given up. That's why it's important to "pile on" as many benefits as you can in your sales letters. The more the reader can see "what's in it for him" the more likely he is to become a customer.

Benefits vs. Features

A feature tells something about the product while a benefit tells how the product affects the reader personally. For example, stating that a stereo has a four-way speaker with high density sound is a feature — it tells something about the product. The fact that the reader can enjoy "true-to-life" rich sounds of music is a benefit. It tells how the product affects the reader.

Let's say you are selling a toaster. How can you possibly make a sales letter sound exciting when describing a toaster? See how transforming product features into benefits helps:

Toaster

Feature	Benefit
15 second toasting cycle	Toasts in just 15 seconds, no long wait to enjoy breakfast; gets you going faster.
Size: 10"x5"	Compact, won't take up valuable counter space.
Adjustable Timer	Enjoy your toast however you want it — warmed up or a crisp dark brown.
Stainless Steel	Durable stainless construction. Shines to a diamond-like gloss. Makes your kitchen more attractive.

As you can see, it's perfectly all right to combine a feature and a benefit. In fact, for products where size and power are important, it may be better to combine the two.

Why People Buy

Psychologists tell us that people buy to satisfy certain human needs. When we are infants, our needs center around survival — getting enough food, water and shelter. But adult needs are much more complex and center around a need to gain. Gain what? People buy to gain:

1. More wealth
2. Better health
3. Better appearance
4. Increased popularity
5. More comfort
6. Greater security
7. More enjoyment

The more your sales letters can tie in to one or more of these motivators, the more effective your letter will be.

Sales Letter For Mobile Pet Bath

Dear Dog Owner:

You may be harming your dog when you give it a bath!

That's right! You can actually irritate your dog's skin by overbathing or using pet shampoos containing harsh skin irritants. Most dog shampoos sold in stores contain Zalik — a known irritant that can cause scaling skin and redness.

But now, thanks to our new mobile pet shampoo service, you can have a clean dog while providing soothing aloe vera lotion to its coat.

We are Mobile Pet Bath and we come straight to your home and shampoo your dog right in our clean mobile facilities. You no longer have to drive your dog to the pet shop, leaving it all day long, cooped up in a cage.

To acquaint you with our convenient service, we are offering our $17.95 shampoo special for only $9.95. This special includes shampoo, an aloe vera rub down and flea treatment.

Please call now for an appointment.

Sincerely yours,

Sales Letter For Collection Service

Dear Business Owner:

Are you spending more to collect past due accounts than you are getting back?

With the expense of personnel, telephone calls, postage, paperwork and overhead, many firms are finding they are spending more than what they are taking in.

But now you can get professional collection services that get results for less than what you're spending doing it yourself.

What's more, we guarantee we will collect more than you

do. That's because this is our *only* business — we are experts in collecting past due accounts.

Best of all, there is no charge for our collection services! If we don't collect on your overdue accounts — you don't pay. We take a small percentage of the amounts we collect.

To introduce you to our collections service, we are offering special collection rates for a limited time. To take advantage of this special offer, simply give us a call.

Sincerely yours,

Sales Letter For Shoe Store

Dear Friend:

Have you ever slipped your feet into luxury? I mean, shoes with all-leather insoles ... all-leather linings!

Most people haven't — these luxuries cost big dollars nowadays. In most stores you would pay $75 to $150 a pair.

But not if you buy from Shoe Warehouse!

Our all-leather shoes are the finest quality. Ordinary shoes have a cork filler between the inner and outer sole. Shoe Warehouse shoes have no filler. Instead, we put in a layer of foam cushion — which is 92 percent air. Our shoes are so flexible, so soft, they don't even need breaking in. Just put them on for immediate comfort and sure custom fit.

You risk nothing by trying a pair of these exclusive all-leather shoes. Wear them for a full 10 days. Compare them for comfort, looks and fit with any other shoe at any price. If they are not the best value you've ever seen, return for a full refund. You'll receive every penny back — no questions asked.

Stop by today — we have a pair of these premium shoes waiting for you.

Sincerely yours,

Sales Letter For Shoe Insert

Dear Foot Sufferer:

Stop putting up with the pain and discomfort of foot pain.

Thousands of foot sufferers like yourself have found relief with Dr. Rollins shoe inserts.

With Dr. Rollins inserts your feet no longer feel the pounding of each step. Instead, they are cradled by the patented cushioned insole enclosed in a genuine leather casing. You've got to feel it for yourself to believe the comfort you'll experience.

If these shoe inserts sold for $200 a pair it would be a bargain. But the price is not $200, $100 or even $50. The price is only $19.95 — a small price to pay for all the relief you'll experience.

Dr. Rollins shoe inserts are being offered on a 30-day free trial. Just call the toll-free number to place your order. You must be 100 percent satisfied with the inserts or return for a full refund.

Now, freedom from foot pain costs you only $19.95. Order Dr. Rollins shoe inserts now while you're thinking about it. You'll be glad you did.

Sincerely yours,

Sales Letter for Telephone Wiring Service

NOW ... SAVE BIG ON TELEPHONE
AND DATA WIRING ... INSTALLATION ...
ADDITIONS ... MOVING ... UPGRADES

Dear Friend:

Ever notice how business people shop around for almost every product and service to get the best possible deal?

Then, when it comes to telephone or data wiring services, they go directly to the telephone company and pay top dollar.

I ask you, does that make sense? When right now my company can handle all your needs and do it at about half what Pacific Telephone charges.

Just take a look at the chart below and see for yourself how much I can save you on hourly charges over Pacific Telephone.

	Pacific Telephone	Budget Connections
First Hour	$74.00	$38.00
Additional Hr.	$48.00	$38.00
After Hours	More $$$	$38.00
Materials	More $$$	Our Cost

And that's just the beginning of how much you can save. After work is completed to your satisfaction, my licensed and professional staff will check over your entire communications system and show you how you can realize big savings on your present monthly costs. These are things that the telephone company knows but probably won't tell you about unless you specifically ask

What's more, my firm can even help you train your own staff to maintain your communications equipment, saving even more money ... month after month. And if you need communications support, I can arrange that too — at the lowest possible cost to you.

Frankly, I can't understand why any business would have work done without first checking on our low prices. I have saved San Diego area businesses hundreds of thousands of dollars in telephone and communications costs. (I'm not bragging, but please look at the enclosed brochure and see how satisfied other San Diego businesses have been with my company's services).

Here's what I want you to do:

- If you need telephone or data wiring services sometime soon, call me right now at 824-222-5409 for a free quotation and consultation.

- If you think you'll need my services sometime in the future, please fill out the enclosed card stating when you want me to contact you to discuss your needs.

Sincerely,

Soliciting Business

Dear Mrs. Lewis:

It has been over six months since you visited us at Covert Corner. We have missed seeing you.

Anything wrong? Please let us know if this is the case.

If you have a chance, why not stop in to see us. I think you will be pleasantly surprised by some of our new merchandise. As a preferred customer, you will be entitled to a ten percent discount on all merchandise.

We stand ready to serve you.

Yours truly,

Offer To Visit Health Spa

Dear Ms. Peppy:

Costa La invites you to a free visit to our health spa and physical fitness center.

Come and enjoy our famous body wrap, tone up with our exercise classes, take a sauna, sample our swimming pool and jacuzzi, bathe in our mineral baths and work out in our gym. I haven't even mentioned our tennis and racquetball courts!

We are very proud of our facilities and would love to show them to you. Please take advantage of our offer. Just stop in and bring this letter with you. We do hope you will come.

Cordially,

Welcome Letter That Solicits Business

Dear Mr. and Mrs. Sloan:

It is a great pleasure to extend our welcome to you. We hope your recent move to Florida brings you much happiness.

If you have never lived in this type of climate before, you may not be aware of the damage our high level of humidity can cause to your fine furs.

We strongly recommend furs be kept in cold storage vaults which provide protection from heat and humidity as well as moths, fire and theft. It costs so little for good protection. Our storage facility offers around-the-clock security in temperature and humidity controlled, fireproof vaults.

You may bring your furs to us, or if you prefer, call us to arrange insured pick-up service.

We are looking forward to serving you.

Sincerely,

Welcome Letter That Solicits Business

Dear Mr. and Mrs. Samuelson:

It is our pleasure to welcome you to the city of Cloveville. You have certainly chosen a lovely area to buy your new home.

As our way of welcoming you, we have enclosed a gift certificate that entitles you to 10% off the regular price of carpet and upholstery cleaning. We are fully equipped to shampoo or steam clean, deodorize and scotchguard your carpets, giving special attention to trouble spots.

We hope you will give us the opportunity to show you the fine work we do. Simply come in or call for a free estimate.

Sincerely,

Congratulations Letter That Solicits Business

Dear Ms. Daisy:

It was with great pleasure we read of your recent engagement. Please accept our congratulations.

Rossies provides a free consultation service for brides-to-be and we invite you to come in to see our exquisite wedding gowns. We specialize in bridal parties and have gowns for bridesmaids, flowergirls and mothers. We also carry a full line of tuxedos which can be purchased or rented.

We hope you will come and visit us.

Sincerely yours,

Birthday Greetings That Solicit Business

Dear Mr. Maison:

Our records indicate that two years ago you purchased a bicycle for your son, Leon, for his birthday.

If he is ready for a larger bicycle, you may wish to surprise him on his upcoming birthday with one of the beautiful models we presently have available in our shop.

We do offer a modest trade-in allowance and will be happy to deliver the bicycle to your home in order to keep it "under wraps" until that special day.

Give it some thought and if you feel Leon should have a new bike, come in at your convenience and I will show you our wide selection.

Cordially,

Recommendation For Preventive Maintenance

Dear Mr. Zara:

Before the hot summer is upon us, we are recommending

our customers call us to arrange a thorough inspection of their air-conditioning systems.

Throughout our many years of experience, we have learned that by taking certain preventive measures such as correcting a minor electrical problem, costly repairs and replacement of parts can often be avoided. Another reason is during the summer we are inundated with service requests. When this occurs, we are unable to provide quick service to all our valued customers.

Won't you give us a call so we can ensure you a cool, comfortable summer?

Sincerely,

Congratulations On New Business Letter That Solicits Business

Dear Mrs. Tilly:

Congratulations on the opening of your new gallery.

We know every business requires a good bookkeeping system. We have developed complete programs for businesses of all sizes. They all have a mutual goal: to minimize paperwork, conserve time spent on bookkeeping, and provide a simple format for keeping records in good order.

I have enclosed our brochure and price list. Upon request, I will be happy to arrange a convenient time for one of our salesmen to meet with you at your location.

Best wishes for your success.

Cordially yours,

Buy Now — Get Billed Later

Dear Mrs. Kary:

Wouldn't it be nice to buy all of your gifts this holiday season without worry about paying for them until March?

We thought it would, and decided this would be a perfect way to thank our customers for shopping with us throughout the year.

Starting today, any purchases charged to your account will not appear on your statement until March 1. This offer is available until Christmas Eve.

We hope you will take advantage of this special offer.

Sincerely,

P.S.   While in the store, come to the third floor for a complimentary glass of eggnog.

Chapter 12

Other Business Letters and Forms

Some business letters do not neatly fit into a specific category. The topics of these letters are endless, from a request for permission to reproduce a magazine article to declining to invest in a business venture. Sometimes you can modify a letter to create one that suits your needs. Other times you can select certain parts of unrelated letters to create a new letter. A little ingenuity and "mix and matching" paragraphs and sentences can produce amazing results. The following letters on various topics might be just what you are looking for.

Thank You For Referral of Client

Dear Mr. Giovanni:

Jack Valent has retained me to represent him.

During our initial conference, he informed me that he has chosen our firm based upon your recommendation. I want to thank you for this referral and inform you I believe we will be able to assist him in this matter.

I am pleased that everything has worked out so well for you.

Cordially,

Thank You For Favorable Comment On Product

Gentlemen:

Thank you for allowing the favorable comment about our product to be broadcast during the airing of "Queen for a Day."

We know this unsolicited endorsement could have easily been deleted from the telecast and we just wanted you to know that it was awfully nice to hear.

I guess I will just have to stay tuned to NSB from now on!

Sincerely,

Thank You For Praising Product

Dear Mrs. Viper:

Thank you for your kind comments on the performance of our product. So few people take time to let a manufacturer know when they are satisfied with a product. Your letter has been sent to Japan where it will be translated to Japanese and posted on the employee bulletin board.

Don't be surprised if you get a few thank you letters from the employees. They pride themselves in the quality of their work and love to hear from customers.

Cordially,

Thank You For Praise For Article

Dear Mr. Kyle:

Thank you for your comments. A copy of your letter has been forwarded to the author for his response. I am sure you will be hearing from him in the near future.

I am pleased you found our article informative and hope you will continue to read our publication. Should you have any comments or questions in the future, please do not hesitate to write to this office.

We value your readership and are proud to have you as a member of our family of subscribers.

Cordially yours,

Welcome To New Tenant

Dear Kelly,

It is our pleasure to welcome you as a tenant of Lakeview Apartments.

We hope you enjoy the fine facilities we offer, including the swimming pool, sauna room, gymnasium and tennis court.

We request your guests use our guest parking area in order to avoid any inconvenience to the other tenants.

Thank you for selecting Lakeview and we sincerely hope you find your new home comfortable and enjoyable. If we can be of any assistance, please let us know.

Cordially,

Request For Help In Locating Someone

Dear Mr. Koran:

For some time I have been unsuccessfully attempting to locate an individual who was previously in your employ.

His name is Todd Banks and I have been informed he worked for you during 1981. If you know his current whereabouts, I would appreciate your either informing me or forwarding this letter to him.

Thank you very much for your help in this matter.

Cordially yours,

Decline To Invest In Business Venture

Dear Mr. Hanks:

Thank you for sending the information on National Campgrounds.

While I found the concept interesting, I am reluctant to become involved in any venture requiring my absence from the firm for an extended period of time.

I am returning your material under separate cover and wish you the best in your new venture.

Sincerely,

Letter To Hotel Authorizing Charges For Guest

Dear Mr. Kelly:

Robert Bruce is an honored guest of our corporation and during his stay at your hotel, you are authorized to forward all bills to our accounting office. They have been preauthorized to immediately approve and pay any invoices from your hotel. We have placed a credit limit on the account of $9,600.00. Should the account exceed that amount, please contact this office for approval in advance of any additional charges.

Thank you for your special consideration of this individual and his needs. We hope to make his visit to our company and our city most enjoyable and memorable.

If I may be of any assistance in this matter, please contact my office.

Yours cordially,

Request For Permission To Reproduce Article

Dear Mr. Zipler:

An article entitled, "Mail Order," written by James Box appeared in the March issue of *Dollar Magazine* which we found both informative and applicable to our business.

We are requesting permission to reproduce an abstract

from this article, with the appropriate acknowledgment, to be used in our current brochure.

If this meets with your approval, would you please send us a notice of authorization.

Sincerely yours,

Denial of Request To Use Name In Advertising

Dear Mr. Tomlinson:

Your letter requesting use of our firm name in your print advertising campaign has been given to me for consideration.

While we have been pleased with the service you have provided and are a satisfied customer, it is against the policy of our company to authorize the use of our name in conjunction with any other product or service.

Therefore, I must refuse your request.

Although it may be a small consolation, we have always spoken well of your product when direct inquiries have been made, and will continue to do so in the future.

If I can be of assistance to you in any other way, please let me know.

Yours truly,

Decline To Allow Use of Name As Charity Sponsor

Dear Mr. Carsono:

Please accept my apologies for having to decline the use of my name as a sponsor of Earth Rights. I feel uncomfortable about sponsoring something I have not put my energies into. I now work with a few charities and I just do not have time to add any more at this moment.

Your cause has merit. I wish you well in your search for prominent names for your sponsor's list. Thank you again for asking me.

Cordially yours,

Denying Job To Friend of Business Acquaintance

Dear Mr. Mactils:

Having been away from the office for a few days, I didn't read your letter of May 19th until today.

While I am sure the young man you wrote me about wouldn't warrant the recommendation you gave unless he is truly exceptional, I believe it unfair to him to set up an interview at this time.

We have just had to lay off twenty-four employees and there is no way I could justify hiring someone new under those circumstances. We anticipate business will improve over the next six months, but for now, the timing is off.

I am sorry to disappoint you. You know, under the right circumstances, we are always looking for bright young people with potential.

Thank you for thinking of us.

Respectfully,

Thanks for Help While Ill

Dear Martha:

Heart attacks are something that happen to the next fellow, and it was therefore rather surprising to wake up in County General Hospital and be informed I had just had one.

I have learned of the generous support you lent to my family during my illness, and would like to sincerely thank you for the kindness and assistance you provided during my immobility. Individuals like you are few and far between.

I am looking forward to returning to work as soon as I get my "clean bill of health." Thank you again.

Many thanks,

Request To Be Excused From School Exam

Dear Professor Wilson:

My employer, Carson Casting Products, is requiring me to attend a company sales meeting in Chicago the entire week of June 4. I strongly asked to be excused because of the examination scheduled for your class on June 6, but my employer declined.

Professor Wilson, would it be all right with you if I took the examination at another time convenient to you? I know you have stated several times that you frown on scheduling make-up tests and I realize this may pose an inconvenience to you. But, my employer is adament that I attend the sales meeting—and I have no alternative but to attend.

Please give my request your thoughtful consideration. I can take the exam whenever and wherever it is convenient for you.

Respectfully,

Authorization To Participate In Medical Plan

As an employee of _____ , I do (do not) wish to participate in the company's medical plan.

_____ is hereby authorized to make the necessary deductions from my earnings or any disability benefit paid to me by the company, for the amount specified in the Group Insurance Schedule.

It is my understanding that I will be eligible to participate in the company medical plan as of _____ and that the monthly deductions referred to herein will begin on _____. I further understand that the acceptance of my application for participation in the Company Medical plan is contingent upon my ability to meet the medical requirements determined by _____.

Date: _____ Signature: _____

Business Credit Application

Business Name _____ Date _____

Address _____ City _____ State _____ Zip _____

Owner/Manager _____ Tel. No. _____

How long in business _____ D&B Rated _____

Trade References:

Name _____ Address _____

Name _____ Address _____

Name _____ Address _____

Name _____ Address _____

Bank References:

Name _____ Address _____

Name _____ Address _____

Credit line requested $ _____

Pending lawsuits against company:

_____

_____

_____

Consumer Credit Application

Name _____ Date _____

Address _____ City _____ State _____ Zip _____

How long at address _____ Own or Rent? _____

Employed by _____ Position _____

How long _____ Salary $ _____

No. dependents _____ Type car owned _____ Year _____

Other sources of income:

_____ $ _____

_____ $ _____

Outstanding obligations:

_____ $ _____

_____ $ _____

Pending lawsuits _____

Have you filed bankruptcy within the last 6 years? _____

Credit references:

Name _____ Address _____

Name _____ Address _____

Bank references:

Name _____ Address _____

Checking _____ Savings _____

Visa Card _____ MasterCard _____

American Express _____ Other Credit Cards _____

_____   _____
Applicant's signature   Date

Consignment Agreement

This agreement is made on _____ between _____ , herein referred to as "Seller,' and _____ .

Whereas, _____ wishes to sell _____ by consigning said item(s) to _____ for sale, it is understood:

That Seller agrees to display item(s) in a prominent place in his establishment.

That Seller will make every attempt to obtain the best possible price for the consigned merchandise and will accept no less than $ _____ as purchase price.

That for his efforts, Seller is entitled to retain _____ % of the purchase price.

That should a sale be effectuated, Seller shall forward a check for the amount of the full purchase price less the aforementioned _____ % to Consignee within 10 days of the receipt of same.

That Seller represents that he maintains insurance for theft and damage, and that the consigned merchandise will be covered by said insurance while it is in his possession.

That consignee agrees to leave the merchandise with Seller for a minimum of _____ .

That should the merchandise remain unsold at the end of the consignment period and an election be made by the Consignee to remove said merchandise, any costs incurred by the delivery of same to Consignee shall be borne by Consignee.

Signature _____ Date _____

Signature _____ Date _____

Acknowledgement of Unsolicited Ideas

Dear Smart:

We appreciate your interest in submitting to us an idea or a proposal relative to: _____

Our firm receives many ideas, suggestions and proposals, and has many of its own projects under development. Therefore, it is possible the idea or proposal you plan to submit to us has been considered and/or may already be in the planning stages.

Nevertheless, we would be pleased to accept your idea or proposal for review, provided it is accompanied by this acknowledgement letter signed by you.

It is understood that:

1. Samples or other submissions will be returned to the submittor only if return postage or freight is prepaid.

2. The company accepts no responsibility for casualty or loss to samples in our possession.

3. The company can accept no responsibility for holding any information in confidence.

4. The company shall pay compensation only in the event it (a) accepts the idea; (b) has received the idea only from the submittor, and (c) reaches agreement with the submittor as to terms and conditions.

If these terms are acceptable to you, please sign where indicated below and return together with your idea or proposal.

Very truly yours,

The foregoing terms and conditions are understood and acknowledged.

_____
Submittor

Pre-Employment Checklist

Date: _____

Applicant: _____

Position: _____

References Requested: Date Received:

_____   _____

_____   _____

_____   _____

Interviewed By: Approved By:

_____   _____

_____   _____

_____   _____

Education verified: _____

Licensure or certification verified: _____

Bonding company approval: _____

Starting Salary $ _____

Fringe Benefits: _____

_____

Effective starting date: _____

Media Survey

How did you learn of our product?

A. Television Commercial? ☐ Yes   ☐ No

   If yes, which channel? _____

   When? ☐ Morning

       ☐ Afternoon

       ☐ Evening

       ☐ Late Night

B. Radio Spot? ☐ Yes   ☐ No

   If yes, which station? _____

   When? ☐ Morning

       ☐ Afternoon

       ☐ Evening

C. Newspaper? ☐ Yes   ☐ No

   If yes, which one? _____

D. Store Display? ☐ Yes   ☐ No

   If yes, which store? _____

E. Other: _____

Chapter 13

Social Letters

Writing a social letter is like making an personal visit by mail. It can be your personal representative when you can't be there. A simple letter can bridge a long distance between people. It can bring friends closer and enrich social relationships. A letter can say thanks for an act of kindness. It can give encouragement to someone experiencing a difficult time in life.

Social letters can go a long way to enrich your life. You can meet people by letter, make friends or even keep love alive. The ability to write social letters can be as important as the ability to speak.

Sure, you probably could pick up the telephone to convey your message and this is most appropriate in many cases. But there is something very special about expressing yourself in writing — taking care to say just the right words to make the impression you want to make.

The reader feels very special that someone has taken the time and effort to compose a letter just for him or her. The letter recipient can read the letter over and over again. A verbal message lasts but a brief moment, but a letter lasts forever.

Selecting Stationery

Social or personal stationery is generally smaller than business stationery — and men and women often use a different size paper.

Men normally use personal stationery measuring 7 by 10 inches or 7½ by 10½ inches, which is the standard Monarch size. Women very often use smaller paper size, 5½ by 7½ inches or 5½ by 6½ inches.

Standard size business stationery (8½ by 11 inches) can be used if you are writing to a company or an individual and not in a business capacity.

Very informal personal correspondence, for example, to close family members or close friends, can be any size within the bounds of good taste. It is a good idea to avoid extremes in size, shape, color and style. Writing paper should not have lines.

Paper used in social correspondence should be white, off-white or pastel color. Always buy a good quality paper because it will make a better impression — plus it is more practical than cheap paper. Better quality paper is easier to write on and holds up better during the beating it will take in the mail system.

Envelopes should match the paper in quality and color.

Selecting the Letterhead

Most printers in your neighborhood can assist you in selecting your letterhead. As with the size of paper, there normally is a difference in the letterhead used by men and women. A man's letterhead generally contains his name, full address and telephone number, although the telephone number is optional. A single woman's letterhead would be the same except the telephone number generally would not appear. If she wanted her telephone number to be known to the reader, she could insert it.

A married woman's letterhead would say "Mrs." with her

145

husband's last name. On very informal correspondence she would use her first name and husband's last name without "Mrs." Single women should omit "Miss" or "Ms." on the letterhead.

The same guidelines apply whether the letterhead is hand-written or typed.

When a personal letter is more than one page, use the same color plain paper for subsequent pages.

Making Letters Look Attractive

Remember that the letter you write is your personal repre-sentative, so be sure it makes the same good impression as a face-to-face visit. That means it should look neat, clean and attractive.

An important aspect of the attractiveness of personal letters is the margins, spacing of the lines and folding.

Spacing

Handwritten letters should be well spaced to enhance read-ability and appearance. A well spaced letter simply is easier to read and looks more inviting to the eye.

Typewritten letters can be single-spaced with double spaces between paragraphs. Letters that are short can be double-spaced with triple-spacing between paragraphs.

Margins

Whether your letter is written by hand or typed, it should look balanced and fit nicely on the page.

If your letter is to be typewritten, try to estimate its length so you can center it on the page. A letter that is grossly off-center does not look attractive and does not make a good impression. Typed letters that fill the entire page shoud have a margin of at least one-and-a-half inches on the top, bottom and both sides. Shorter letters should have corresponding wider margins so the letter looks balanced on the page.

Personal letters generally should be written on one side only, especially if they are typewritten.

Folding The Letter

Most personal letter paper should fold once to fit neatly into the envelope. Make sure the edges are even and attractive looking. A carelessly folded letter may not make a favorable impression on the reader.

Letters needing more than one fold to fit into the envelope should be folded in three equal sections and neatly placed in the envelope.

The Essential Parts of A Social Letter

Personal and social letters should consist of five parts as follows:

1. **The Heading**
   Your address and date

2. **The Salutation**
   Your opening greeting to the reader, i.e., Dear Sally

3. **The Body of the Letter**
   What your letter says

4. **The Close**
   Where you say goodbye to the reader

5. **The Signature**
   The writer signs the letter in ink

Personal letters do not have an inside address as do business letters. Also omitted in personal letters is the typed signature and special notations such as initials of the letter writer and typist.

The salutation of a personal letter has a comma after it unlike a business letter which has a colon.

The Complimentary Closing

There is a wide variation in the complimentary closing for letters to friends and loved ones. You should use one that you feel comfortable with. Some commonly used closings are:

Best regards,

Warm regards,

Warmly,

Fondly,

Forever yours,

Your friend,

Thank you,

Many thanks,

Thanks again,

With appreciation,

Affectionately,

Yours affectionately,

Love,

With love,

Much love,

Lots of love,

All my love,

Lovingly,

Love and kisses,

Missing you,

Each complimentary closing implies a varying degree of friendship or close, loving relationship. You should never use a closing you don't really mean. For example, you shouldn't use "Yours affectionately," if you can bearly tolerate that person. Nor would you use "Your friend," if you didn't consider that person a real friend.

Personal letters should be written in ink and, of course, be signed in ink. It normally is not considered in good taste to write a letter in pencil.

Handwritten vs Typewritten Letters

While the typewriter is being used more for personal correspondence, a handwritten letter or note is much more personal and intimate. Short notes should normally be handwritten — especially thank you notes, sympathy notes and invitations. Most other types of social correspondence can be typewritten or handwritten as you prefer.

Social
Models

The social letters in this book will get the results you want and make the right impression. When you need a certain kind of social letter, simply refer to the table of contents and select the appropriate letter. You can copy the letter word-for-word or use it as a guide to create your own letter. Often a minor change of a word or two can give you just what you are looking for. Other times you may want to take a sentence or two from one letter and additional sentences from other letters — creating your own letter.

Chapter 14

Letters of Announcement and Introduction

When a happy event occurs in your life, a letter is a perfect way to spread the good news. The announcement could be for the birth of a baby, engagement or a child coming to live with you. Many people send announcements to friends upon the opening of a new business.

Announcements should be brief and cover only news about the happy event.

When you believe two people would enjoy each other's company, you may consider sending a letter of introduction. For example, if you have a friend who is visiting a city where you have another friend — and you believe it would be mutually enjoyable for them to meet — you may want to write a letter of introduction. A letter of introduction is normally mailed but can also be presented personally by the person being introduced.

A letter of introduction should give the name of the person being introduced, the reason for the introduction and other information on why a meeting would be appropriate. The letter should include an expression of appreciation for the courtesies requested of the recipient.

Announcing A Baby

Dear Louise,

I am proud to announce the birth of my brand new son, Paul James. He was born June 17 at 7:35 p.m. He weighed 6 pounds even and was 21 inches long.

We are so thankful he is healthy, handsome and happy.

Fondly,

Announcing A Baby

Dear Raymond and Tisha,

Bob and I have a new addition to the family — and she is gorgeous. Her name is Machell Maril. She was born October 5 at 6:15 a.m., weighed 9 pounds, 9 ounces and measured 23 inches.

With the three boys, we are elated to now have a healthy little girl. We are sending pictures.

Much love,

Announcing an Engagement

Dear Uncle Lester,

I wanted you to be one of the first to know that I'm engaged to be married.

His name is James Robert Digenerat. He is 37 years old and is vice president of the Midland National Bank. He believes in family and wants a large one as I do.

Uncle Lester, he is exactly the kind of man I've been searching for all these years. I couldn't be happier. I plan to drop by soon so you can meet him.

Lovingly,

Announcing A Divorce

Dear John and Mary,

I wanted you both to know that Norman and I have

divorced. We tried to work out our differences, even sought professional help, but to no avail. We both agreed it would be better to go our separate ways.

My new address and telephone number is listed above. I hope this won't in any way affect our friendship.

As ever,

Announcing A Divorce

Dear Polly,

This will probably come as a shock, but Kelvin and I have recently divorced. I started working again at Finnies and have my own apartment in Georgetown. You can get in touch with me at the above address and telephone number.

Cordially yours,

Announcing A New Business

Dear Friends,

I am announcing today the opening of 24-Hour Typing Service. As the name implies, most typing can be completed and returned within one day. And since all material is entered on a BTI-400 word processor, changes can be made easily and quickly.

So the next time you need typing done, just call me. You'll find my rates are the lowest around.

Cordially yours,

Announcing A Business

Dear Neighbor,

I'm pleased to announce the opening of Jake's Landscaping Service. As you may know, I've been doing lawn maintenance in the neighborhood for several years now — on a part-time basis. Because of my growing number of satisfied customers, I've decided to make it a full-time business.

If you're doing your own yard maintenance, or you are not happy with your present arrangement, give me a call. I have dozens of references in your neighborhood.

Sincerely yours,

Introducing Daughter

Dear Neighbors,

I am pleased to introduce my daughter, Julie Ann, who will be living with me.

Julie Ann is twelve and will be attending the seventh grade at Harper Junior High School. She loves sports and has participated in junior varsity track and volleyball. She was also on the debate team.

She is looking forward to meeting everyone in the neighborhood.

Sincerely yours,

Introducing New Neighbors

Dear Mr. and Mrs. Busybody:

I would like to introduce your new neighbors, Robert and Barbara Boyari, who just moved in at 6214 Luana Avenue.

The Boyaris have relocated from Boston where they owned and operated a successful restaurant chain. They plan to take about a year off before getting into another business.

Over the next several weeks, I hope you can meet Robert and Barbara.

Cordially yours,

Introducing New Neighbors

Dear Mrs. Busybody:

I'm delighted to introduce my new neighbors, Geraldine and Oscar Coznowski.

The Coznowskis moved here from Detroit, Michigan after working at the Ford Motor Company for thirty-one years. Geraldine was Chief Administrative Assistant for domestic sales and Oscar was a Maintenance Supervisor. They both love sports, especially tennis and golf. Geraldine is involved in several national projects to help the homeless.

The Coznowskis did not relocate here to retire. Instead, they plan to open a Polish restaurant sometime in June. Oscar will do the cooking while Geraldine will manage the table service.

I hope you will join me in making the Coznowskis feel welcome. I know you will enjoy meeting them as much as I did.

Cordially,

Introducing A Friend

Dear Wally,

My brother-in-law, Joe Pernicone, will be visiting San Diego the first week in June to give a speech before the American Radiological Society. I've always wanted you both to meet —and this seems like a great opportunity.

Joe is a practicing radiologist and one of the leading authorities on magnetic resonance imaging (MRI). Since you plan to specialize in MRI, I thought you both would enjoy talking over dinner one night. I believe you would have a lot in common.

Wally, if you are available, call him — he is staying at the Cozy-Flats Hotel. I'm suggesting this meeting only because I believe you both would benefit.

Cordially,

Hand-Delivered Letter of Introduction

Dear Mr. Creeps:

This letter will introduce Carlos Vinciani, a very good friend of mine. Carlos will be in Detroit for six months on special assignment for his employer, Fox Industrial Associates.

Carlos is a fine young man and I feel certain you will enjoy his company. He has never been in Detroit and would appreciate any advice you could provide on restaurants and sights to see. I'll be very grateful for any help you could give him.

Very truly yours,

Chapter 15

Letters of Congratulations

When something special happens to a relative, friend or neighbor, consider sending a letter of congratulations right away. A special occasion could be graduation from school, receipt of an award, a promotion, delivery of a great speech, a new business venture and so on.

The written message should be brief and focus entirely on the happy event. Discussing other matters would only detract from the special occasion.

A brief note of congratulations will go a long way to enhance personal relationships as well as making the recipient feel terrific about his or her accomplishment.

Congratulations — Graduation

Dear Wilma,

Congratulations on receiving your master's degree in psychology from Michigan State University. This is quite an accomplishment. I know it took years of work and hard study on your part, and it's an achievement you can be very proud of.

Uncle Bill and I have followed your progress with much interest and pleasure. You know you have made us both extremely proud.

Whatever you seek to undertake in the future, we know you will be successful. Our very best wishes go out to you.

Warmly,

Congratulations — To Parents Upon Graduation of Son

Dear Andrea,

We read in the paper today that Tom graduated from Ferris State College with high honors. You must be very proud of his accomplishments and we are very happy for you. I'm sure Tom worked hard and long and he deserves every bit of the praise he must be getting.

Please give Tom our heartiest congratulations and our very best wishes for happiness and success in future endeavors.

As ever,

Congratulations — Graduation

Dear Frank,

Heartiest congratulations on your graduation from Sudman High School. A job well done! Your mother tells me you plan to attend Miami University in the fall. Best of luck to you in the future.

Best regards,

Congratulations — Award

Dear Ronald,

Congratulations for receiving the Outstanding Citizen Award from the City of Detroit. It's a fine tribute you richly deserve for your heroic efforts in rescuing two elderly women from a blazing house fire.

As I understand it, you were the top part of a three man "human ladder" formed to reach up to the window where the women were screaming for help. Upon reaching the window, you single-handedly grasped each woman and lowered her down to safety. All this was done in total disregard for your own safety while flames and smoke shot out of the window.

159

I want you to know everyone is extremely proud of what you did and it would be a better world if more people had the courage and bravery you displayed.

Best wishes,

Congratulations — Successful Business Venture

Dear Ned,

I picked up *Success Magazine* today and saw your picture on the cover with your Spartan Motorcar.

The inside article was very complimentary of your efforts to make the car company a success. I was particularly impressed with how you started virtually from scratch and with hard work and perserverance, made Spartan the premiere luxury sports car in America.

I want to add my congratulations to the many you must be receiving. I wish you continued success with this venture along with the happiness and satisfaction you richly deserve.

Cordially yours,

Congratulations — New Business Venture

Dear George,

I was thrilled to learn your new restaurant, George's Fish House, is open and ready for business. With your experience in food service and proven management ability, I know the restaurant will be a tremendous success.

Congratulations to you, George. I'm so happy that your hard work has paid off.

Best regards,

Congratulations — Promotion

Dear Randy,

I read in this morning's paper that you were appointed to head the downriver office of Middleton Auto Insurance.

My warm congratulations go out to you. I knew it was just a matter of time before your outstanding abilities and hard work were recognized.

I wish you the greatest possible success in the future.

Sincerely yours,

Congratulations — Promotion

Dear Rachel,

I was delighted to learn about your promotion to Vice President. Congratulations! You've certainly earned it, and I know you'll find your new job challenging and stimulating.

Warm regards,

Congratulations — Promotion

Dear Anne,

I was very pleased to hear of your promotion to District Manager of your company. You are extremely talented and you've worked very hard to achieve this goal. I am glad to hear your efforts are being rewarded.

My sincere congratulations go out to you.

Best regards,

Congratulations — Published Article

Dear Peter,

I just read your article "Drugs and Our Youth" in the *Tribune* this morning. Congratulations! I'm happy to see someone has finally zeroed in on the root cause of the problem and suggested solutions that really make sense.

Your outstanding article made a material contribution to the understanding of this horrible problem. Keep up the fine work!

Best regards,

Congratulations — Speech

Dear Carl,

The speech you delivered last night at the Charity Benefit was most inspiring. As you were speaking, I looked around the room and saw every eye "glued" to the podium. Even those who didn't necessarily agree with your position were impressed by the clarity and soundness of your presentation. You must have put a considerable amount of time and research into preparation for the speech.

I want to congratulate you on a job well done! We are all looking forward to the next time you take the podium.

Warm regards,

Congratulations — Speech

Dear Ron,

Let me congratulate you on making one of the best speeches I ever had the opportunity of hearing. The audience was all but spellbound by your perceptive analysis of crime in America. I thought the applause would go on all night.

Your ideas are most thought-provoking, and I want to thank you for sharing them with us. I hope you'll be our speaker again at a future club meeting.

Cordially yours,

Congratulations — Engagement

Dear Jennifer,

We were so pleased when you called last night to tell us about your engagement to Charles. He is a very lucky man as I'm sure he knows. You both must be feeling pretty good about now.

Congratulations to you and Charles. And we wish you all the happiness in the world.

All my love,

Congratulations — Engagement

Dear Pauline,

That's terrific news! I heard from Emily that you and Jeff announced your engagement last night. Congratulations to both of you.

Here's wishing you both a lifetime of love and prosperity.

Your friend,

Congratulations — Engagement

Dear Heather,

I received the exciting news about your engagment last night. You know how happy I am for you. While I haven't had the opportunity to meet Fletcher, from what you've told me, he seems like a wonderful person.

Best wishes from both of us. We hope you will have nothing but joy and happiness in your life together.

All my love,

Congratulations — Marriage

Dear Andy and Zelda,

Congratulations on your marriage. Here's wishing you both

a life of happiness and joy!

Best wishes,

Congratulations — Marriage

Dear Cindy,

It's hard for me to believe you are old enough to be married. It seems like only yesterday you were a little girl with braces on your teeth and pretty braids in your hair.

Give my heartiest congratulations to your new husband, Jim. We can't wait to meet him so we can welcome him into the family.

Here's wishing you both eternal happiness and ever increasing joy as the years go by.

Lots of love,

Congratulations — Marriage

Dear Teddy,

Your Aunt Julie and I are so happy and proud of you for your recent marriage to Carson. You know how fond we are of him. We always knew you would pick an outstanding person like him to spend your life with.

Julie and I both send our love and best wishes for every happiness life can bring.

Affectionately,

Congratulations — Baby

Dear Wilma,

How happy you must be to have a brand new baby girl. I hear she is simply beautiful, even at seven days old.

Frank must be exploding with pride. I know he wanted a girl.

Congratulations to you both. We wish all possible joy and happiness with your new little girl.

Warmly,

Congratulations — Baby

Dear Thelma,

Congratulations on the birth of your son, Calvin. I'm so happy to hear it's a boy for now little Peggy will have that baby brother she's been talking about.

May the years ahead be filled with good health and good fortune for little Calvin and the entire family.

Warmly,

Congratulations — Twins

Dear Barb,

I was so excited to hear of the birth of the twins. Your pleasure and joy has been doubled by two little boys. Sandy told me they both are absolutely handsome and adorable.

Roger and I send our warmest congratulations and best wishes to you, Tom, and the twins.

Best regards,

Congratulations — Wedding Anniversary

Dear Steven and Mary,

Congratulations on your tenth wedding anniversary. It seems like only yesterday that I was best man at the wedding. Where has time gone?

Best wishes to you both for continued joy and happiness.

With love,

Congratulations — Wedding Anniversary

Dear Fred and Wilma,

Charlie and I send you both our warm congratulations on your wedding anniversary. It must be a great source of pride and pleasure to celebrate twenty-six years of marriage.

We wish you both continued happiness and contentment in the years ahead.

As ever,

Congratulations — Wedding Anniversary

Dear Donna,

Sally and I send our sincerest congratulations on your upcoming wedding anniversary. Our very best wishes to both of you now and in the years to come.

As ever,

Chapter 16

Letters of Thanks

When someone has been generous, thoughtful or extremely kind, sending a thank you note should be a pleasurable task.

The thank you note could express appreciation for a special favor, hospitality, a gift, financial help or anytime someone goes out of his way for you. Even though you have expressed your appreciation to a person verbally, you can still send a written thank you note. A written note carries much more meaning and can be read time and again.

Letters of thanks should be sent out as soon as possible and should have a warm, sincere tone.

Thank You For Hospitality

Dear Betty,

I thoroughly enjoyed the gracious hospitality you showed me during my weekend in Clearwater. You went out of your way to spoil me. The meals were meticulously prepared and were absolutely delicious. The dinner at the French restaurant was the best I've ever eaten.

It was terrific getting together with you once again. Keep in mind my standing invitation to let me spoil you the next time you are in Georgia.

Thanks again. You are a dear friend!

All my best,

Thank You For Hospitality

Dear Fred and Norma,

How is it possible to express how much Bob and I enjoyed our week at your ranch. Everything was absolutely perfect: the beautiful surroundings, the terrific weather, and most important of all — your gracious company.

We want you both to know how we appreciate your hospitality and the kindness you have shown us. Bob and I consider ourselves fortunate to have such wonderful friends.

Affectionately yours,

Thank You For Wedding Gift

Dear Jerry and Sally,

Sam and I want to thank you for the gorgeous handmade quilt. You were much too generous.

We plan to have you both over so you can see for yourselves how the quilt brightens up the bedroom.

Thanks again for the lovely gift.

Fondly,

Thank You For A Gift

Dear Brett,

You have an uncanny ability to select the perfect gift. The video you sent me was so terrific, I stayed up half the night enjoying it. How in the world did you find out about my fondness for horror movies? Thank you for a wonderful gift.

Affectionately,

Thank You For Birthday Gift

Dear Uncle Willy:

How did you know I wanted a watch for my birthday? You couldn't have chosen anything better. I love it.

The digital dial is really classy and the band fits perfectly. The white gold matches all my other jewelry.

Thank you, Uncle Willy. You're a real genius for selecting the perfect gift.

With love,

Late Thank You For Birthday Gift

Dear Aunt Jenny,

I've thought so often about writing to thank you for the birthday gift — I'd begun to think I already had. I apologize for taking so long.

I just love the sweater you sent me. The grey is beautiful and goes with most of my other clothes. I've already worn the sweater at least a dozen times.

Thanks again for the terrific gift.

Love,

Thank You For A Gift

Dear Heather,

What a magnificient gift! How generous of you to select such a beautiful lamp for George and me. We were overwhelmed with excitement when we unpacked it this morning. The lamp is sitting on the table as I write this note. I can't stop looking at it and marveling at its unique beauty.

Thank you so much, Heather. We are expecting you to be a very frequent visitor at our house. George says come soon!

With love,

Thank You For The Gift

Dear Judy,

When I opened your gift today, I was so excited. The twelve-piece towel set is just beautiful. How were you able to perfectly match the towels with my bathroom? I can't believe how much the towels brighten up and beautify the place. They are lovely. Thanks so much.

With love,

Thank You For A Gift

Dear Shirley,

The box of chocolates arrived this morning, special delivery. You remembered how much I love Sounddar's candy. You'll have to tell me how you got them to send the candy all the way from Boston. On second thought, don't tell me because I'll be ordering a box every week.

Thank you so much for remembering my birthday.

With love,

Thank You For Baby Shower Gift

Dear Cari,

Thank you so much for the beautiful handmade baby blanket. It must have taken you a long time to make it. I plan to take the blanket to the hospital to wrap the new baby in when we come home.

As ever,

Gift Not Acknowledged

Dear Fred,

In balancing my checkbook this morning, I noticed the $50 check I sent you for your birthday was not cashed. Fred, please let me know whether you ever received the check. If not, I can send off a replacement right away.

All my love,

Gift Not Acknowledged

Dear Joe and Mary,

Hope this letter finds you both as happy as ever and settled in your new apartment.

We are a little concerned that you haven't mentioned the wedding gift we sent you. If it's an oversight, we fully understand. But if the gift never arrived, we'll have to investigate. We sent you a 24-piece blue lead crystal glassware set. The set was shipped from Bronsons to your previous apartment in Glendale.

Please let me know if the set ever arrived. If not, I'll have a replacement sent.

With love,

Thank You For Favor — Watching Dog

Dear Bob,

Thank you so much for taking care of Brea while I was away last week. She is such a lucky dog to be able to enjoy your huge yard. When I picked her up, it was obvious she was well cared for and enjoyed her stay.

Your help is greatly appreciated. I had piece of mind while away and saved money too. Thanks again.

Your friend,

Thank You For Favor — Watching Twins

Dear Al and Annie,

I can't thank you both enough for watching the twins while Bob and I were in Denver. It's wonderful to have great friends whom we can trust with our children. Tommy can't stop talking about the pizza restaurant you took him to. Jimmy liked being able to stay up late and watch television.

I am very lucky to have friends like you. Please accept this gift as a token of my appreciation.

Love,

Thank You For Favor — Caring For Animals

Dear Minnie,

I was able to fully enjoy my weekend ski trip knowing that Tinker and Bennie were being well cared for. Both cats looked so content when I picked them up — I know they got plenty of love and attention.

I can't thank you enough for being such a good friend. And I'm really looking forward to taking care of that gorgeous German shepard, Boo Boo, when you visit your folks next month.

As ever,

Thank You For Favor — Caring For Animals

Dear Dave,

Thanks so much for taking care of Romeo and Tilly while I was in Washington, D.C. Both dogs are so lucky to have you to watch out for them. They absolutely hate the kennel.

I also consider myself lucky to have such a good friend as you.

Please accept this gift I picked up for you at a little shop near the White House.

Thank you,

Thank You For Favor — Use of Beach House

Dear Ned and Joan,

Thank you so much for letting my mother, dad and sister use your beach house last week. They had a terrific time. The weather was near perfect and, of course, your beach house is always so cozy and relaxing.

Frankly, I don't know how I would have made room for the family at my house. Dad would have had to sleep on the couch. It would have been really cramped.

I really appreciate how kind and generous you've been to my family and me. Thanks again!

Fondly,

Thank You For Favor — Help Moving

Dear Ralph,

I just wanted to tell you what a great friend you are for helping me move to my new apartment. I know you are very busy and it was a real sacrifice to take time to help.

I was just looking over the furniture and I couldn't see a single scratch. That's amazing considering the number of flights of stairs we hauled the furniture.

You can be assured that I will take time to help you move anytime, anywhere. Thanks again.

Fondly,

Thank You For Favor

Dear Phillis,

Thank you so much for the tickets to see Tom Jones. Being in the third row, Karen and I could almost reach out and touch him.

The show was absolutely thrilling. Tom sang all my favorite songs plus many new songs I will never forget. Yes, a girl sitting right behind me threw her pants onto the stage.

I really appreciate your thoughtfulness and generosity.

All my love,

Thank You For Favor

Dear Billy,

When my computer stopped working, I thought I had lost six weeks of work. Then you came over and showed me how to get up and running without losing a single piece of data. You are a computer genius and I want to thank you so much for all your help.

Sincerely,

Thank You For Retirement Party

To The Financial Planning Department:

I want to thank everyone for the most wonderful retirement party and terrific set of personally monogrammed golf clubs. I can't think of a more unforgettable way to round off my career at Fedro-Sims.

Twenty-two years of service is a long time and I will take with me many precious memories.

As Ethel and I get ready for our move to Phoenix, I want each and every one of you to know I feel most honored for the privilege of working with such quality people. I consider you all friends.

Affectionately,

Thank You For Retirement Party

To The Plant Layout Staff:

What a memorable way to top off 15 years of service to Casper's Forge Plate. I want to thank everyone for the fantastic retirement party and leather suitcase. The scrapbook you prepared, Joyce, will forever remind me of the great years we all shared together.

I want you all to know I feel very privileged for the opportunity to work with such terrific people. I will miss you all.

Thanks again for everything.

Respectfully,

Thank You For Financial Help

Dear Uncle Alex,

I'm enclosing a copy of my college diploma with the notation "Thank you Uncle Alex! Your generous financial help made this possible." (When I get my first paycheck next week, I'm buying you a nice frame for it.)

How can I possibly thank you enough. I know you are not rich, Uncle Alex, and I know you work really hard for your money. That's why I appreciate so much the help you've given me.

Uncle Alex, I plan to pay every penny back. I know you told me I don't have to, but I have too much respect and love for you not to.

With love,

Thank You For Dinner

Dear Mary,

I want to thank you and Bob for bringing over that terrific dinner yesterday. Henry is still raving about how tender the beef was. That was so thoughtful of you both.

I was so happy to get the night off. It was really hectic bringing the baby home from the hospital and getting her settled in. You both are wonderful and we cherish your friendship.

Thank you,

Chapter 17

Letters of Sympathy

Sympathy letters are often difficult to write for many people. Yet, there is no time when a letter can mean so much and be so deeply appreciated. When someone is going through a difficult time, knowing that another person cares and is available to help can really ease the pain. Sure, a greeting card could be sent, but often only the sender's name is read.

The purpose of a sympathy letter is to comfort. Therefore, the letter should not dwell on details of a death, illness or tragedy. It should not touch on memories that would only deepen the sorrow.

Sympathy letters should be brief and indicate how saddened or shocked you were to learn of the occasion — and how the person is in your thoughts. Close with a final offer to help. Sympathy letters should always be handwritten.

Death of Wife

Dear Randy,

Al and I are sending you our deepest sympathy on the death of your wife, Carol. She will be greatly missed and we join everyone in sharing your grief during this difficult time.

Affectionately,

Death of Wife

Dear Larry,

I just learned with profound sorrow of the death of your wife, Gloria. Our hearts are filled with sympathy for you in this difficult period.

You know if there is anything we can do, you only have to tell us.

With love,

Death of Husband

Dear Lisa,

I am profoundly sorry to learn of the death of your husband, Calvin, and I want you to know how deeply we feel for you in your sorrow. Please call us if there's anything we can do. We would be most honored to help in any way possible.

We send you our love, and assurance of devoted friendship.

All my love,

Death of Husband

Dear Joan,

I sympathize with you, Joan, at the loss of your husband. Our hearts are filled with sorrow. Tom and I wish with all our hearts we could help comfort you in some way. We are standing by to help in any way we can.

Affectionately,

Death of Father

Dear Evan,

All our thoughts are with you at the loss of your father. I had the privilege of knowing your father and he was a kind and generous man who will not soon be forgotten by those who knew and admired him.

I'm sending our deepest sympathy to you and our warm personal regards to your family.

Your friends,

Death of Father

Dear Julie,

My heart is filled with sorrow for you on the loss of your father. I can sympathize with you for my father was taken less than a year ago.

Brad and I are standing by to offer any help or comfort we can. Please call me if there is anything at all we can do.

Sincerely yours,

Death of Mother

Dear Diane,

Words can't express my profound sorrow with the passing of your mother. She was loved and respected by all those fortunate enough to know her. She was a good woman and will be long remembered in the hearts of many.

We send our deepest sympathy.

Forever yours,

Death of Mother

Dear Jack,

Our deepest sympathy goes out to you and your family on the passing of your mother. Pat and I want you to know we are thinking of you. Please let us know if there's anything we can do.

Forever yours,

Death of Child

Dear Carl and Sonya,

There are no words to express the sorrow we feel for you in the sudden passing of your son, Jeff.
Jack and I send our love and deepest sympathy.
We beg you to let us help in any way we can.

With love,

Death of Child

Dear Mr. and Mrs. Caldwell,

Phyllis and I want you to know how deeply we feel for you in this time of sorrow. We were shocked and saddened at the news and our hearts go out to you.

Affectionately,

Death of Relative

Dear Tony,

I just received word of the death of your brother, Ryan. Please count me among those who share your sorrow. It was a privilege to know him. He'll be missed by everyone who knew him.

As ever,

Death of Relative

Dear Mr. Wiseman,

We read in this morning's paper of the death of your sister. We were shocked and saddened by this tragic news, and our hearts go out to you and your family.

We send our deepest sympathy and warmest regards.

Sincerely yours,

Illness

Dear Harry,

I was so sad to hear of your illness, but I'm happy you're resting comfortably and getting good care. I'm sure you'll be up and about in no time at all.

I'm sending you several books on astrology with best wishes for a complete return to health.

Forever yours,

Illness

Dear Ethel,

Fred and I are sending our best wishes for a speedy recovery. You have been on our minds ever since you entered the hospital. We are delighted to hear you are making progress. Keep it up Ethel! And come home real soon to all those who miss and love you.

Missing you,

Accident

Dear Clyde,

I can't begin to tell you how sorry I was to learn of your accident. Your family tells me you are progressing nicely and you'll be out of the hospital in about a week.

I'm sending you every good wish for a speedy recovery.

Best wishes,

Accident

Dear Pamela,

I'm happy to hear you're back home and recovering from the accident. Your brother tells me your doctor was a noted specialist and that you're coming along nicely.

I will be standing by to provide any help you request. Meanwhile, I'm sending along my wishes for a super-fast recovery.

Fondly,

Misfortune — Flood Damage

Dear Clay and Lois,

Words can't express how sorry we were to learn the flood caused considerable damage to your home. Betty and I know how special your home was to you both. If there's anything at all we can do to help, let us know. You are welcome to use our basement for storage until your house is repaired.

Our thoughts and concern as friends go out to both of you.

As ever,

Misfortune — House Fire

Dear Ted and Julie,

Mildred called this morning and told of the fire that destroyed your home. We know how terribly distressing this can be as we lost our home to fire five years ago. We are more than happy to help in any way possible.

All our thoughts are with you both. We are sending assurances of devoted friendship.

As ever,

Chapter 18

Letters of Apology and Regret

Sometimes it is difficult for people to say, "I'm sorry." This is because we sometimes hate to admit we were wrong or made a mistake. Yet, the ability to make a genuine expression of regret shows an inner strength. That strength comes from the ability to swallow your pride for the sake of another's feelings.

The apology should come at the beginning of the letter. The letter shouldn't ramble and give the impression that the apology is made relunctantly. If appropriate, offer an explanation in a clear, concise manner. Try to avoid long, drawn out reasons why something happened or didn't happen.

Always make assurances that you will avoid a reoccurrence — then close the letter on a positive, forward-looking note.

Bounced Check

Dear Phillis,

This morning I received a notice from my bank that the $56 check I wrote you for the stereo bounced.

I just returned from the bank where I deposited more than enough money to cover the check. Please redeposit the check.

Please accept my sincere apology for my oversight.

Thank you,

Poor Behavior

Dear Martha,

I deeply regret what happened at the dinner party last night. I acted like a real fool. I hope you will accept my apology. Believe me, Martha, nothing like this will ever happen again.

As ever,

Missed Lunch

Dear Frank,

There is no excuse for my not meeting you at lunch yesterday. I really goofed! The appointment was written on my calendar and I was looking forward to the occasion. But somehow I thought our date was for next Tuesday. I should have stayed in bed that day because everything went wrong.

Please accept my sincere apology. Believe me, Frank, my face is "beet red." I'll call you before you go to Boston to arrange another meeting at your convenience.

As ever,

Missed Meeting

Dear Lisa,

Please accept my apology for missing lunch Wednesday. As you know, there was a terrible snow storm that day which started about 10 am. I got caught right in the middle of it.

I stopped at a telephone booth and tried to reach you, but you had already left for the restaurant.

At 1:45, I was still about 5 miles from the restaurant so I decided to call it a day and return home. I didn't arrive home until 6:30.

Please accept my apology, Lisa.

Your friend,

185

Broken Lamp

Dear Wilma,

I was very distressed to learn that my son, Oscar, broke your crystal lamp yesterday while "roughhousing" with Jeff. I know the lamp was dear to you and that you're extremely irritated at the boys — with good reason.

I know the lamp can never be replaced. But I've made arrangements to have it repaired at Walter's Fine Lamps. Based on your description of the damage, there's a good chance it can be restored to its original condition.

Oscar will pay for the repair from his earnings at the hardware store.

Best regards,

Loan Not Repaid

Dear Barry,

Today I ran across a crumpled up note in my green shorts. The note was a reminder that I owe you $55. I haven't worn those shorts since Veteran's Day. That means I've owed you $55 for almost five months now. Why didn't you remind me?

I'm sending along a $55 check with my apology for the oversight. Thanks for being such a good friend.

As ever,

Loan Not Repaid

Dear Wally,

Boy, am I embarrassed! I just remembered that I never returned the $90 you loaned me in Las Vegas last month. All the fun and excitement must have clouded my memory.

I'm sending along a check with my sincere apology for the oversight.

Next time I'll bring more money. Thanks again.

With appreciation,

Child Broke Glasses

Dear Mrs. Mactal,

Bonnie came home yesterday with tears streaming down her face. She told me she accidentally sat on Mylene's glasses and broke them. She feels very badly.

I've called Dr. Rolling's office and told him to make an exact duplicate of her glasses. They will be ready Friday. I will pick them up and deliver them to you.

Please explain to Mylene how sorry we are this happened.

Cordially,

Regret — Didn't Attend Meeting

Dear Sam,

I was disappointed not to see you at the Gentlemen's Club meeting last night and wondered what happened to you. You mentioned the day before you planned to attend.

The speaker, Allie Smith, spoke on patriotism and it was inspiring indeed. You would have enjoyed it.

I hope to see you at the next meeting in June.

Cordially,

Overdue In Sending Books

Dear Lucy,

At last I'm sending you the two books on investing that I promised you several months ago. As you know, I just returned from Europe after a several week stay in England.

I found the book entitled "Crisis Investing" to be especially interesting in today's economic environment. The other book is also interesting but advocates a more conservative approach to investing.

I hope you find the books helpful and rewarding.

Cordially yours,

Dog Dug Up Yard

Dear Tim and Cheri,

Mary told you both how sorry she was that our dog, Weasle, dug up your front yard yesterday. I want to express my apologies and let you know it won't happen again.

Weasle chewed the leash that held him to the dog house, then jumped the fence. I just purchased a steel chain leash that can't be chewed off.

Please send me all bills and expenses related to the holes — I will cover them right away.

Thank you for being such good neighbors.

Best regards,

Misunderstanding On Dates

Dear Vanna,

We've been friends for 14 years. Let's not let a little misunderstanding come between us. I thought you said you were going to the Key West with me in January, but you can't remember making that commitment. It's really no big problem. I can get a full refund on both airplane tickets. The hotel has also agreed to give me a full refund.

We are both busy and I'm sorry I didn't make the plans more clear to you.

Sincerely,

Dog Barking

Dear Mrs. Beck,

Thank you for your note telling of my dog Fang's constant barking on Saturday. I was gone most of the day and had no idea he was being an annoyance. I certainly do not want to disturb you, especially with the new baby. I know how annoying a barking dog can be.

To make sure this does not happen again, I plan to put Fang in the garage if I'm gone for more than two hours. Then if he does bark, you won't be able to hear him.

I sincerely hope this will never happen again. If it does, let me know right away and I will take stronger measures to quiet Fang.

Cordially yours,

Dog Scratched Boy

Dear Mrs. Adams,

I'm so sorry that our dog, Bentley, scratched your son, Mark, Saturday. The boys were playing baseball in the back-yard and Bentley loves to chase the ball. I guess he got over-anxious and jumped on Mark's back.

I immediately cleaned the scratches with peroxide and covered them with salve — so there should be little cause for concern about infection.

Bentley was punished right after the incident and the boys have agreed to play ball at the park. So this should never happen again.

Best regards,

Chapter 19

Invitations

Today, most social invitations are informal and require only a simple note or a letter of invitation.

An informal invitation to a dinner, luncheon or party should be addressed to the wife alone, for herself and husband (the invitation should specifically mention the husband). The envelope is addressed to the wife but with the husband's first name — Mrs. James Black.

The invitation should clearly indicate the occasion, the location, the date and time. Most informal invitations are handwritten and sent out at least a week before the occasion.

A formal invitation is used for an elaborate function, like a church wedding, ceremonious dinner, an important reception or dance. Formal invitations are generally engraved, but can also be handwritten. Formal invitations are not indented like regular letters. Instead, they are arranged in a decorative irregularly indented format. (Examples are shown in this chapter) Formal invitations are written in the third person and are sent out at least two or even three weeks in advance. Wedding invitations are generally mailed a month in advance.

Dinner Invitation

Dear Jennifer,

Will you and George have dinner with us on Thursday, the third of June, at seven o'clock?

We haven't gotten together for a while and want to hear about your trip to China.

Cordially,

Dinner Invitation

Dear Carla,

Paul and I are having some close friends here for dinner on Tuesday, April four, at seven o'clock. Of course the get-together wouldn't be complete without you and Tom.

We sure hope you can come. We haven't gotten together for some time now. We miss you both.

We are looking forward to seeing you.

Warmly,

Dinner Invitation

Dear Mrs. Jackson,

Richard and I would be very happy if you and Mr. Jackson could join us for dinner on Friday, the twelfth of November.

Dinner is at seven o'clock. We sure hope you can come.

Sincerely yours,

Dinner Invitation

Dear Mr. Celery,

Roger and I are wondering if you could come to dinner on Sunday, the fourth of February.

I hope you'll be able to come. Dinner is at seven.

Cordially yours,

Dinner Invitation

Dear Cindy,

We are having an informal buffet dinner Saturday afternoon, July seventh. Of course we want you and Dennis to be there.

Come over at about three. The Wallaces and Barrys are planning to come. After dinner, we can play a few hands of cards.

We are looking forward to seeing you.

Affectionately,

Dinner invitation

Dear Walter,

I know you are interested in rare automobiles, so I thought of you when I invited the Lemmons to dinner next Wednesday the third. The Lemmons own a Spartan II Motorcar which they plan to drive to our house.

We are planning dinner at about seven. Why don't you come about six so we can take a good look at the car.

Looking forward to seeing you.

As ever,

Engraved Invitation to Formal Dinner

Mr. and Mrs. Arnold Swatts
request the pleasure of your company
at dinner
on Friday, May the fourth
at nine o'clock
126 Willow Street
Big Rapids

Engraved Invitation to Formal Luncheon

Mrs. Foster James Flover
requests the pleasure of your company
at luncheon
on Monday, February the thirteenth
at two o'clock
Costa La Club
Del Mar, California

Engraved Invitation to Formal Dance

Mr. and Mrs. Donald Thump
request the pleasure of your company
at a dance
on Saturday, the seventh of June
at half after nine o'clock
50 Gulfside
Indian Rocks

Recalling Dinner Invitation

Dear Cheri,

I have just learned that Jerry's mother has taken ill. We are driving to Cleveland tomorrow morning. Although she is 83, the doctors say she will recover.

We therefore regretfully recall our dinner invitation for Thursday, the fourth of August.

We will plan another dinner at a later time. Please forgive this last-minute change.

Yours truly,

Recalling Dinner Invitation

Dear Pat,

I am very disappointed to have to cancel the dinner planned for Thursday, the fourth of April. After Paula came down with the chicken pox, John and I decided not to expose our friends to her contagious condition.

Please forgive us for this last-minute change of plans, but I'm sure you understand.

Once Paula recovers, we plan to reschedule the dinner.

As ever,

Luncheon Invitation

Dear Joyce,

If you are free next Wednesday, the sixth of June, will you join Robert and me for luncheon?

Is twelve o'clock too early? We are looking forward to seeing you. I hope you can join us.

As ever,

Luncheon Invitation

Dear Jim,

Professor Robbins is dropping by for the day next week. As you know, we both had him for our advanced accounting course at Farriss Business School.

I know he would be delighted to see you. If you are free Monday, June seventh at noon, please join us for a luncheon at my house.

We will be looking forward to seeing you. I hope you can come.

Sincerely yours,

Luncheon Invitation

Dear Eileen,

Will you come to my luncheon on Friday, April the tenth, at eleven o'clock?

My brother, Ronald, will be visiting from Detroit. I know you both will have a lot in common.

I hope you can come.

As ever,

Theater and Dinner Invitation

Dear Judy,

I'm holding in my hand four tickets to a special showing of *Silver Fox*, starring James Reed, for Wednesday, July second at eight o'clock.

Why don't you and Rex join us. I know how much you both enjoy James Reed.

We could pick you up on the way to the theater. Let me know if you have other plans. Otherwise, we'll pick you up at seven.

Affectionately,

Card Party Invitation

Dear Peggy,

Rudy and I are having a bridge party this Saturday, February second at eight o'clock. The Carsons and Smiths are coming. They are terrific players.

Why don't you and Robert plan on coming at about seven so we can chat before the others arrive.

We'll be looking forward to seeing you both.

Warmly,

Cocktail Party Invitation

Dear Emma,

We're having some friends over for cocktails, Friday, March seventh, at six o'clock. We sure hope you and Perry can come.

Ralph and I are looking forward to seeing you both.

Warmly,

Barbecue Party Invitation

Dear Bertha,

Bill and I are having an informal barbecue in our backyard on Saturday, July fifth, at noon. The Wilsons and Becks are coming. It would be so nice if you and Lester could come. The entrees are chicken and ribs.

Hope you both can come. We'd love to have you!

Warmly yours,

Pool Party Invitation

Dear Robert and Elaine,

To celebrate completion of our pool, we are having a pool party this Sunday, June fourth, at one o'clock. The Bores and Deadpets are coming. We sure hope you can come.

Bring your bathing suits. Looking forward to seeing you both.

As ever,

Shower Invitation

Dear Miss Witty,

I am having a wedding shower for Karen Queen on Friday,

February second, at four o'clock. I sure hope you can come. A four-entree buffet will be served.

Karen has often mentioned you as a friend and roommate at college. She would be delighted if you could come.

I am looking forward to the pleasure of meeting you.

Cordially yours,

Christening Invitation

Dear Ron and Kathy,

Our daughter is going to be christened at the American Church on Sunday, June four, at nine o'clock. We would be so pleased if you both would come to the service.

Sincerely yours,

Children's Party Invitation

Dear Mrs. Bower,

We are having a birthday party for Bobbie this Friday, November the fifth, at four o'clock. Bobbie would be so happy if Cindy could come.

Of course we will play plenty of games and award prizes. Afterwards, ice cream and birthday cake will be served.

We are looking forward to seeing Cindy at the party.

Warm regards,

Children's Party Invitation

Dear Candi,

My mother is having a birthday party for me Saturday, June tenth, at one o'clock. I sure hope you can come, Candi. I'm looking forward to seeing you.

Your friend,

Family Reunion Invitation

Dear Janey,

Paul and I are planning a family reunion party at Hines Park, Saturday, August the third at one o'clock. We are providing all the chicken, hamburgers and hot dogs. Bring your own refreshments and other food items.

We are placing plenty of signs from the main roads so finding the party shouldn't be a problem.

About fifty family members are expected to come. We do hope you can join us.

Warm regards,

Chapter 20

Acceptance
of Invitations

An invitation is a compliment and deserves a prompt and gracious response. Your acceptance note should express pleasure at being invited. It should also repeat essential details of the occasion such as the date, day of week and hour. This assures the host there is no misunderstanding or confusion about the event.

Your reply to the invitation should be the same style as the invitation you receive. This is particularly important when responding to a formal invitation.

Dinner Acceptance

Dear Patti,

George and I will be delighted to have dinner with you and Ted on Thursday, June third, at seven o'clock. How very thoughtful of you to write us.

We are looking forward to seeing you.

Warmly,

Dinner Acceptance

Dear Denise,

How nice of you to invite Tom and me to dinner Tuesday, April four, at seven o'clock. We will be delighted to come and are looking forward to the occasion.

Warm regards,

Dinner Acceptance

Dear Mrs. Forbes,

Thank you for inviting Richard and me to dinner on Friday, November twelve. We would be most honored to come.

We are looking forward to seeing you both at seven o'clock.

Yours sincerely,

Dinner Acceptance

Dear Thelma,

Roger and I were very pleased to receive your invitation to dinner on Sunday, February four, at seven o'clock. How nice of you to ask.

Of course we will come. We are looking forward with pleasure to seeing you both.

As ever,

Luncheon Acceptance

Dear Sandy,

Wally and I appreciate your invitation for luncheon Wednesday, June the sixth.

We are looking forward with delight to seeing you both at noon.

As ever,

Luncheon Acceptance

Dear Allen,

I was pleased to receive your letter asking me to luncheon with you and Professor Robbins.

I will be delighted to come Monday, June the seventh, at noon.

I am very much looking forward to seeing you both.

Yours sincerely,

Luncheon Acceptance

Dear Randy,

Yes, I will come to your luncheon on Friday, April the tenth, at eleven o'clock.

I am looking forward with pleasure to seeing you and your brother, Ron.

Warmly,

Theater and Dinner Acceptance

Dear Anne,

I cannot tell you how delighted Phil and I were to receive your invitation to the James Reed concert on Wednesday, July second, at eight o'clock.

Of course we will come. You know how crazy we are about James Reed.

We'll be waiting for you to pick us up at seven. Thanks for being so thoughtful.

Warmly,

Card Party Acceptance

Dear David,

Rudy and I would love to come to your bridge party this Saturday, February second, at eight o'clock. We welcome the challenge of playing the Carsons and Smiths.

We'll be there at about seven so we can plan our strategy.

We're looking forward to the occasion. Thanks again for inviting us.

Fondly,

Cocktail Party Acceptance

Dear Connie,

Thanks so much for inviting us to your cocktail party, Friday, March seventh, at six o'clock. We wouldn't miss it for the world.

We are looking forward to the occasion with great pleasure.

Fondly,

Barbecue Party Acceptance

Dear Irene,

How nice of you to invite Lester and me to your backyard barbecue Saturday, July fifth, at noon. We accept with pleasure and are looking forward to seeing you, the Wilsons and Becks.

Thanks again for being so thoughtful.

Fondly,

Shower Acceptance

Dear Mrs. Kilo,

Thank you so much for inviting me to the wedding shower for Karen Queen this Friday, February second, at four.

I accept the invitation with great delight. Karen and I were college roommates and remain best of friends today.

I am looking forward with pleasure to the occasion.

Cordially yours,

Children's Party Acceptance

Dear Mrs. Tyson,

Cindy says she will be delighted to attend Bobbie's birthday party this Friday at four o'clock. She is so excited. Thank you so much for inviting her.

Warm regards,

Chapter 21

Declining Invitations

When you cannot accept an invitation, express your disappointment and give the reason for not accepting. Refusal letters should leave the recipient with the impression that the invitation was most welcome and flattering and is turned down with genuine regret. No other topics should be covered — only matters relating to the refusal.

Regret replies should be in the same style as the invitation received, especially when replying to formal invitations.

Dinner Regret

Dear Patti,

I'm so sorry we can't come to dinner on Thursday. We just found out George's father is in the hospital again. We are leaving tomorrow to see him.

Thank you so much for inviting us, Patti. We always enjoy your company and are disappointed about missing the occasion.

Affectionately,

Dinner Regret

Dear Denise,

We just received your invitation to dinner this Tuesday. I wish we could come because we always enjoy your dinner parties. But Dan and I had previously made plans to spend that weeek in Las Vegas.

We are both very sorry we can't make it this time. But thanks so much for thinking about us. We hope to see you both real soon.

Forever yours,

Dinner Regret

Dear Mrs. Forbes,

Thank you so much for asking Richard and me to dinner Friday. We wish we could accept but we are expecting guests ourselves that night. What a shame because we really enjoy your company.

It was so thoughtful of you to invite us. Let's keep in touch and get together another time soon.

Forever yours,

Dinner Regret

Dear Thelma,

Many thanks for your thoughtful invitation to dinner this Sunday. Roger and I will be out of town that day. Remember I told you we were going skiing at Big Top that weekend?

We are both very disappointed we can't make it. We really enjoy your company and always look forward to your dinner parties.

Fondly,

Luncheon Regret

Dear Sandy,

It was so kind of you to ask Wally and me for luncheon this Wednesday. We really appreciate your thinking of us.

Unfortunately, we must drive our daughter, Carolyn, to Julian that day to start summer camp. We are so sorry we can't accept your kind invitation. I hope you will ask us again real soon.

Warmly yours,

Luncheon Regret

Dear Allen,

I wish I could accept your invitation to luncheon with you and Professor Robbins this Monday. Unfortunately, I have a previous commitment. One of my key clients is coming in from Washington to discuss a major contract.

I am really disappointed because I was looking forward to seeing you both. But thanks so much for thinking of me. I really appreciate the kind invitation.

Cordially yours,

Theater and Dinner Regret

Dear Anne,

I'm so disappointed I could cry. Phil and I must decline your invitation to see the James Reed concert this Wednesday.

We made a previous commitment to close the deal on the summer cottage at Lake Tahoe. We are flying there Tuesday and returning Friday.

Anne, it was so wonderful of you to invite us to the concert.

Phil and I will never forget your thoughtfulness. Our very best to you and Willie.

Forever yours,

Card Party Regret

Dear David,

Your welcomed invitation to the bridge party this Saturday came this morning. Thanks so much for asking us. We always enjoy your company.

We would love to come, but Rudy and I promised to help a friend conduct a grand opening for a new Tasty Jack restaurant. We made the commitment over six months ago.

We are so disappointed because we always enjoy your bridge parties. We appreciate your thinking of us and are looking forward to another occasion.

Best wishes,

Cocktail Party Regret

Dear Connie,

I wish I could accept your invitation to the cocktail party this Friday. But as luck would have it, I'll be out of town for a company sales meeting. Thank you for thinking of me. I hope I'll be available next time. Best of luck to you and Tony.

Fondly,

Shower Regret

Dear Mrs. Kilo,

I wish I could accept the invitation to the wedding shower for Karen Queen this Friday. Unfortunately, I will be out of the country that week. Karen and I have always been close and I feel badly about not being able to attend.

Thank you so much for thinking of me. Best of luck to you.

Cordially yours,

Children's Party Regret

Dear Mrs. Tyson,

Cindy has the mumps and won't be able to attend Bobbie's birthday party this Friday. She is so disappointed. Thank you so much for inviting her. Cindy sends her love and kisses.

Best wishes,

Chapter 22

Letters Asking A Favor and Requesting Information

The secret to getting results from letters requesting favors is explaining to the reader in a convincing manner the reason for the request. Whenever possible, tell the reader how he may benefit from your request. Better yet, offer the reader something in return. Sometimes it helps to explain to the reader why you came to him or her.

When asking several questions in one letter, it's a good idea to number the questions. This way you're more likely to receive specific answers to each question.

Make the reply easier by providing a self-addressed envelope. This will greatly increase your chances of getting a response.

Asking A Favor — Look After Dog

Dear Peggy,

I would like to ask a tremendous favor of you.

Is there a chance you could look after my dog, Boo Boo, for the entire month of July? You've offered to watch him several times in the past.

I have a chance to tour Europe during July at a special discounted rate. It's a chance of a lifetime!

Peggy, I realize this is asking a lot, but you know I will return the favor whenever I can do something to help you.

Warm regards,

Asking For A Job For Relative

Dear Walter,

As I mentioned at Tuesday's luncheon, I'm enclosing the resume of my grandson, Lester Gesseppi.

Lester is a fine young man displaying intelligence and a good deal of integrity and ambition. He was recently discharged from the Army after a three year tour of duty in Germany where he made sergeant.

Walter, could you please see if you can find a suitable job for him in your company? You know you can call on me anytime I can return the favor.

Many thanks.

As ever,

Lining Up Speakers

Dear Carla,

The monthly luncheon for Formerly Fat Women is coming up on July 14. I'm trying to put together a list of speakers. Can you help me?

As manager of the Forever Fit Spa, would you be willing to contact several women who have lost a substantial amount of weight? I'm trying to line up at least three women guest speakers. Each guest would speak for about ten minutes on how they were able to slim down and then keep the weight off.

I would really appreciate any help you could give me.

As ever,

Finding A Guest Speaker

Dear Mr. Lucci,

As one of the top salesmen in the state, would you be willing to spend about 20 minutes with our Sunday School group discussing your methods and techniques?

The group of 15 young men and women, between the ages of eight and ten, formed last year to sell handmade potholders. The proceeds will provide needed money to a family who lost their home in a recent fire.

The group is young, but very enthusiastic. They would be most excited if you could talk to them April seventh, at 6:30 pm at the Weaverly Center.

Please let me know. I can make arrangements to pick you up.

Respectfully yours,

Letter Requesting Extension of Time on Guarantee

Dear Mr. Brodmore:

Is it possible to get a 30-day extension on the moneyback guarantee for my Reliable X-14 model computer. The original guarantee was 90 days from date of purchase.

Unfortunately, my software was not completed until 60 days after I purchased the X-14. This leaves me only 30 days to test the computer.

The performance so far has been excellent, but an additional 30 days of testing would tell me for sure whether the computer suits my needs.

Please respond as soon as possible. Many thanks.

Cordially yours,

Letter Requesting Extension of Time

Dear Mr. Thak:

I'm enclosing a copy of my option on the rental space at Thak's Storage. The option expires November 30.

My mother, who lives in Boston, is very ill and I may have to return there for an extended period. I'll have a better picture of her condition by the end of December.

Would it be possible to extend the option renewal date to January 15? I would really appreciate it.

Cordially yours,

Request to Revise Contract

Dear Mr. Bozot:

We contracted with your firm to install a pool beginning July 1. Since signing the contract, our financial condition has taken an unexpected turn for the better. As a result, we are requesting that you begin work on June 1.

If the earlier starting date is possible, please revise the completion date on our contract and send me a copy for signature.

Thank you so much.

Cordially yours,

Request For Favor — Start Car

Dear Raymond,

Thank you so much for sending me the cheerful get-well card.

You asked whether there was anything you could do. It was very kind of you to offer and I hope you don't mind my saying, "Yes, there is!"

Would you please start my car about twice a week? The key is under the side doormat. Let the car run for about 15 minutes. I would really appreciate your help.

I plan to be up and about soon and will be anxious to return the favor.

As ever,

Request For Written Copy of Speech

Dear Mr. Harmon:

I attended the spring conference of the American Association of Helping Hands and was most impressed with your outstanding presentation on the homeless problem. I've never seen such a captive audience — I thought the applause would go on all night long.

I wonder if you have a written copy of your talk that you could send me. I want to review all your points with the objective of implementing them in a personal help plan.

I'm looking forward to hearing from you soon.

Respectfully,

Request For Financial Data

Dear Mr. Cheatum:

I'm being audited by the IRS on August 15 and need a schedule of all my stock and bond transactions for the year ending December 31. For each transaction I need:

— Date of purchase and price
— Date of sale and price, and
— Brokerage fees.

I need the information by August 1 so my accountant can review the transactions before the audit date.

Your prompt attention will be greatly appreciated.

Sincerely yours,

Request For Information

Dear Mr. Jelly:

I am preparing a paper entitled, "Computers of the Future" for my Master's program at Wayne State University.

Since National Computers is one of the foremost computer companies in the world, I'm requesting any information you may have on this subject. This includes internal reports and studies or any outside material you can direct me to.

Many thanks for your kind assistance.

Cordially yours,

Request for Information

Gentlemen:

I am planning to relocate to Clearwater in the near future. Please send me any information you have regarding business opportunities for a laundromat.

Any information you can provide will be greatly appreciated.

Sincerely yours,

Request for Information

Dear Staff,

The terrific article in the June issue entitled "Zinc and the Prostate" mentioned zinc may be helpful in alleviating prostate symptoms. Could you please tell me what dosage is recommended and what form of zinc gets the best results.

I will be anxiously awaiting your response. I really enjoy the magazine. Keep up the good work!

With appreciation,

Information On Housecleaning Service

Gentlemen:

I noted your advertisement for housecleaning with a good deal of interest. I'm very curious how an average-size home can be cleaned in one hour flat.

Would you please send me details on your housecleaning service including the cost of cleaning windows.

Sincerely yours,

Request for Information

Dear Mr. Babico,

I am considering installing a Bell 314 computer to maintain my mailing list of about 5,000 customers. Jack Farber told me you have used a 314 for almost a year now.

Could you please help me by briefly answering the following questions:

1. Have you found the Bell 314 reliable?
2. How would you assess the support quality?
3. Would you recommend the 314?

Thank you so much. I sincerely appreciate your help.

Warm regards,

Request For Free Booklet

Dear Mr. Hall:

Could you please send me a complimentary copy of "How to Avoid The Five Biggest Home Buying Traps." I understand the booklet is very useful, especially to first-time home buyers.

Many thanks for your kind assistance.

Respectfully yours,

Credit Card Application

Gentlemen:

I am considering opening a charge account at your store and would appreciate your sending me an application.

I look forward to hearing from you soon as I plan to start Christmas shopping early this year.

Cordially,

Locating A Book

Gentlemen:

I am trying to find a copy of Robert Cartwright's book "Reason For Living." It doesn't matter if the book is new or used. I understand the book was published by Emerson Press, but is now out of print.

If you have a copy, please send it C.O.D. Or, you can call me collect and charge it to my credit card.

Thank you.

Yours truly,

Request For Catalog of Products

Gentlemen:

I purchased a Zeno stereo about 16 years ago and it has given me outstanding service. Now I'm ready to buy another stereo.

Would you please send me a catalog of your newest Zeno stereo systems and the names and addresses of authorized dealers in my area.

I'm thanking you in advance for your prompt attention to this request.

Cordially,

Subscribing To A Publication

Gentlemen:

I'm enclosing a $26 check for a year's subscription to the "Monthly Agriculture Report."

Also put my name on your mailing list for other government publications dealing with farming.

Yours truly,

Add Name To Mailing List

Dear Sirs:

Would you please add my name to your mailing list for the publication "Monetary Reports." I understand the publication is issued monthly and is a free service offered to Americans over the age of 35.

Many thanks.

Cordially yours,

Chapter 23

Letters to Neighbors

There may be times when it is better to write a letter to a neighbor rather than to have a face-to-face confrontation. You and a neighbor may have had harsh words over an issue and you want to avoid a heated argument. Or, the neighbor may work different hours than you so it's difficult to get together for a talk.

Sometimes it may be appropriate to send an unsigned letter to a neighbor. You may want to consider this when you know a neighbor is a "hot head" and would be outraged at bringing a problem to his or her attention. In this situation, an unsigned letter would avoid possible violence. Letters to neighbors should be signed in most instances.

Stereo Too Loud

Dear Neighbor,

Almost every night — starting about 5:30 in the evening —your stereo blasts through the wall making my life almost unbearable. The wall vibrates, the floor shakes and the furniture rattles. I can hardly rest, relax or think.

As you know, the walls between the condo units are almost paper thin. Any little noise goes right through to other units.

The other day, I went to your unit and talked to your son, Ray. He was very polite and said he would turn the volume down. This helped somewhat — but the noise level is still too loud.

I realize you have every right to enjoy your stereo. But please keep in mind I'm on the other side of the wall hearing nothing but thump . . . thump . . . thump . . . .

I believe the solution to the problem is to move the stereo to another wall. The north wall seems like a good choice since, being an end unit, the stereo noise would echo out toward the garden area.

I know you are a good neighbor and will give my problem your prompt consideration. I really appreciate your kindness.

Thank you,

Dog Jumping Fence

Dear Mrs. Falkin,

Your dog, Flicker, is making a habit of jumping the fence and coming over to my backyard.

I don't mind Flicker coming over once in a while. He is company and plays nicely with my dog, Bowser. But for the last month, he has been over every day.

The other day, I had to cover up several holes Flicker dug. The holes around the flower bed were especially troublesome since several new plants were destroyed. Flicker also likes

219

chewing on articles of clothing I hang out to dry.

I noticed that Flicker gets over the fence by first jumping on the large pot by the fence. I believe if you moved the pot, he would be unable to leap up high enough to get over the fence.

If there's anything I can do to help solve this problem, please let me know.

Cordially yours,

Return Borrowed Lawn Mower

Dear Charlie,

You're hard to get hold of now that you're working full time! I've gone over to your house at least five times in the last two weeks but you've been at work or sleeping.

Yesterday, I asked your daughter, Jill, if I could have my mower back since my grass hasn't been cut in a while. She said it was locked in the shed behind your house and she didn't know where the key was.

Charlie, now that you're back to work, I would appreciate your making arrangements to buy or rent your own mower. You have borrowed mine steadily for almost two years now. I believe I've been more than generous. What's more, Charlie, I feel you're taking advantage of my good nature.

Please return my mower as soon as possible so I can cut my grass before the homeowner's association gets on my back.

Thank you,

Odor From Dog Piles

Dear Mrs. Bailey,

For weeks I didn't know where that horrible smell was coming from — then I looked over the fence onto your backyard.

I couldn't believe my eyes. Sitting in your yard are dozens and dozens of dog piles. There are more piles than grass.

The smell is particularly bad when we have a westerly wind. Mrs. Bailey, sometimes the smell is so bad I am forced to hold my breath when I pass by the fence. Even worse, the smell often comes through the window and creates a foul odor throughout the entire house.

I know that once I bring this matter to your attention, you will take corrective measures — so I won't be forced into filing a complaint with the city.

Yours truly,

Pool Pump Too Loud

Dear Mary,

I've been waking up to the clang of your noisy swimming pool pump for the last month now. This is particularly nerve-racking on the weekends when I would prefer sleeping in.

When the pump was new, I could hardly hear it. But as the rubber cups wear out, the pump noise increases. I have my cups replaced every nine months before they get noisy and possibly do permanent damage to the pump's internal mechanism.

I would be happy to give you the name and telephone number of the person who maintains my swimming pool. He is reliable and very reasonable.

However you decide to repair the pump, I would appreciate if you could do it as soon as you can.

Thank you,

Barking Dog

Dear Mr. Samuelson,

Last night was the third time this week that your dog, Wolf, woke me and Joyce up in the middle of the night. As you know, I get up for work at five in the morning and drive a long distance to the city. Joyce gets up with the baby at night and gets very little sleep.

Do you think you could keep Wolf in the garage at night? I've noticed he doesn't bark when he is in the garage. Joyce and I would really appreciate it. I'm thanking you in advance for your prompt attention to this matter.

Cordially yours,

Someone Parks In Your Reserved Space

Dear Mr. Jameson,

It seems whenever you have a party, one of your guests parks in my reserved space. Last night was the fourth time in four weeks this has happened. A blue Nissan, license plate #6216, was parked in my clearly marked space.

Instead of taking someone else's space, I parked four blocks away on Evans Street. But this is the last time — I've had it.

The next time I find a car parked in my spot, I'm calling Jerry's Towing. It will cost the owner of the car $60 to get the car back. I've checked with the Palmdale Police and having an unauthorized vehicle towed from a reserved parking space is perfectly legal.

Let's save us both time and aggravation. Tell your friends not to park in my reserved space.

Thank you,

Compliment Parents For Honest Child

Dear Mr. and Mrs. Covington,

While your son John and his friends were playing baseball yesterday, a hard ball was hit through my living room window. Once the ball shattered the window, all the boys scattered —except John. He came to the door, admitting responsibility and offered to pay for the broken window with earnings from his hardware store job.

I was very impressed with John's honesty. He is a fine boy. You both should be commended for instilling such a sense of responsibility in him. I hope the boys will be more careful in the future.

Sincerely,

P.S. Tell John this one's on me — honesty pays!

Zoning Violation Warning

Dear Occupant:

You are operating a car repair business out of your home in violation of city zoning ordinances.

Sometimes there are four, five and even six cars parked in your driveway awaiting repair. This creates an eyesore for the entire neighborhood, not to mention the noise and people crowded around your front yard.

Moreover, the increase in street traffic created by your business places the children on the block at an increased risk. Just the other day one of your customers had to slam on the brakes to avoid hitting a little girl.

One of the costs of doing business is the rent for space in a location zoned for commercial, not residential use. The convenience and low cost of running a business from your home is at the expense of others — your neighbors.

Please don't force me to report this matter to the city zoning commission. Your prompt action is appreciated.

Signature Optional

Abandoned Car in Driveway

Dear Occupant:

That blue 1972 Oldsmobile has been sitting in your driveway for almost three years now. As far as I know, it has never been moved. The windows are so dirty you can't see the inside of the car. It is not a pretty sight.

I believe three years is ample time to decide what to do with the car. Why don't you consider having it repaired or selling the car? Anything is better than just letting it sit in your driveway.

The entire neighborhood is waiting for you to do something with the abandoned car in your driveway.

Signature Optional

Too Many Cars Parked In Driveway

Dear Neighbor,

The front of your house looks like a used car lot. At any time, day or night, there are between 4 to 6 cars parked in front of your house. At least two of the cars seem to be abandoned in the driveway. Only three of the cars appear to be driven regularly.

The whole neighborhood would appreciate your "weeding out" some of the nonworking vehicles. This would go a long way to improving the appearance of our street.

Signature Optional

Clean Up Front Yard

Dear Neighbor,

The next time you drive up to your house, take a good look. Notice how tall your grass is — at least six inches. See the color of the grass — an ugly brown caused by months of neglect. Look at the shrubs — dying and uneven from lack of water and care.

Only you can improve the appearance of your front yard. It wouldn't take much — just a little water, fertilizer and good old-fashioned hard work.

The entire neighborhood is anxiously awaiting to see some improvement in your lawn. Why not be a good neighbor and do something now.

Signature Optional

RV Parked On Street

Dear Neighbor,

The huge 21 foot motor home parked in front of your home is a real eyesore.

Few people would mind if the motor home was parked there on a temporary basis, such as between weekend trips. But the motor home seems to be a permanent neighborhood fixture. I don't believe it has been moved for at least six months.

As you may know, city ordinances require that vehicles be moved every 24 hours. When is the last time the motor home was moved?

I don't want to contact the city about this matter. But if you don't find some other place to park the motor home, I'll be forced to do so. Please be reasonable so we can avoid further problems.

Signature Optional

Need To Paint House

Dear Neighbor:

The shabby appearance of your home has forced me to write you this letter.

When you moved here five years ago, the home was in near perfect condition. But with the passing years, the paint has all but worn away from the wood. This diminishes the beauty of the home and leaves the wood subject to deterioration.

A simple coat of paint would do wonders to beautify your home and improve the general appearance of the neighborhood. Your neighbors would all appreciate your prompt attention to this matter.

Signature Optional

Thank You for Loan of Car

Dear Jim,

When my new car wouldn't start this morning, I thought for sure I would miss the job interview. You were much too generous in offering me the use of your car. I was right on time for the interview. And guess what? I got the job!

Thanks again for your kindness.

Thank you,

Chapter 24

Letters of Complaint

When you are not satisfied with a product or service, write a letter of complaint. You will probably feel better because you were able to vent your dissatisfaction and the company will be happy to know of a problem with its product or services so it can take corrective measures.

Very often a letter of complaint results in a positive benefit to you. For example, dissatisfaction with a meal often results in an invitation to come back to a restaurant for a free meal. Writing a large manufacturer with a complaint often brings coupons for complimentary products.

A complaint letter should provide all essential details about your unhappiness and state what action or adjustment you expect. Your letter should sound level-headed and objective.

Nonreceipt of Product

Dear Customer Service Staff:

On August 14, I sent you a check for $39.95 for an electronic flea repellant collar for my dog. As of today, November 16, I have not received the product I ordered.

I know you received the order because you cashed my check on August 23 (copy of both sides of cancelled check enclosed).

It's been over two months since I ordered the flea collar. Either ship the product immediately or issue a prompt refund.

Thank you for your help.

Cordially,

Returned Product — No Refund Received

Dear Customer Service Staff:

On February 2, I ordered a bottle of your EverYoung skin lotion. I returned the lotion on February 21 for full refund as stated in your money-back guarantee. As of April 4, I have not received my refund. Please look into this and issue my refund as soon as possible.

Cordially yours,

Rebate Check Never Received

Dear Customer Service:

On about January 4, I purchased a Quality coffee maker with a $20 manufacturer's rebate offer. A few days later I sent you the cash register receipt from the store, the rebate certificate on the bottom of the box and the completed rebate form.

As of March 21, I have not received the $20 rebate.

I'm enclosing a copy of my sales receipt. Please send my rebate immediately.

Thank you,

Requesting Refund From Travel Agent

Dear Ms. Wilson:

In late November, I sent you a $100 deposit check for a Paradise Cruise to Bermuda for the week of February 2.

Due to an injury to my back, I will be unable to go on the cruise. I am enclosing a letter from Dr. Carson.

Please refund my $100 as soon as possible.

Thank you.

Cordially yours,

Cancelling A Door-To-Door Sales Contract

Dear Mr. Jameson:

This certified letter is to advise of my cancellation of the order I placed with you yesterday for the Hurricane vacuum cleaning system.

According to the State Consumer Protection office, there is a 3-day "cooling off" period on door-to-door sales. During this period, the contract can be cancelled without recourse or penalty.

For your information, after I slept on the purchase of the vacuum, I decided my present vacuum is more than adequate for my needs.

Please don't contact me with reasons why I should change my decision. My mind is made up.

I'm sorry for any inconvenience this may have caused you.

Thank you,

Restaurant Shortchanging Customers

Dear Mr. Amerstating:

As owner of Amerstating's Barbecue Restaurant, I want to bring to your attention a serious problem with your cashier, Jimmy. The last three times I ate at your restaurant, Jimmy tried to shortchange me.

The first time I didn't notice until I got home. I was short-changed $2. The next time I was shortchanged $1. I immediately informed Jimmy. He said he was sorry for an "unintentional mistake." The last time I was shortchanged $5. Again he apologized for the "mistake." These three occasions happened within a three week period during July.

Common sense would dictate that either Jimmy is very poor in math or he is trying to hustle your customers.

Either way, I urge you to investigate this matter promptly

before it adversely affects the reputation of your excellent restaurant.

Sincerely yours,

Charge Account Billing Error

Dear Billing Staff:

Please be advised of the discrepancy between my monthly statement and charge receipt issued by the merchant (copies enclosed).

As you can see, the sweater purchase was for $117.56. But the charge statement shows $171.56.

I'm making the correction on my monthly payment. Please correct your records as soon as possible.

Thank you,

Merchandise Returned — Want Refund

Gentlemen:

I am returning the waist belt I purchased on July 7 for $10.95. Your catalog states that merchandise can be returned for full refund within 30 days.

The waist belt was comfortable to wear, but did not hold my stomach in as advertised. Therefore, after three day's use, I am taking advantage of your money-back guarantee.

Please make the refund check payable to Lois Watson, and sent it to Anders, California 92033.

Thank you.

Cordially,

Charge Account Error

Gentlemen:

My June credit card statement contains a duplicate billing

for Dick Fanny Health Club membership dues.

On June 14 there is a charge for $108. The identical charge appears on June 18, as you can see from the enclosed statement.

Please credit my account for the duplicate $108 charge. I'm deducting that amount from the enclosed check.

Thank you.

Cordially yours,

Delivery Not Made — Waited All Day

Dear Mr. Dingle:

On April 4, I purchased a solid oak five-piece bedroom set from your store. The salesperson assured me the set would be delivered on Friday, April 7.

I waited all day Friday, cancelling other plans. At 4 pm the furniture still hadn't arrived. I called the store and was told by Mr. Tomer, the Warehouse Manager, that the set was never placed on the truck for delivery.

When I purchased the bedroom set, I told the salesperson how important it was to have the set delivered on Friday because I was leaving on vacation the following Tuesday.

I am very upset about this mix up.

My husband and I have decided to cancel the order. I am expecting a full immediate refund of my deposit.

Sincerely,

New Car Problem

Dear Mr. Reasoner:

I purchased a new Cardinal automobile from your dealership on October 7. I paid cash for the car and drove it home that same day after a cursory inspection.

Once home, I gave the car a more thorough inspection finding several minor problems. As each day passed, however, I noticed more problems with the car. It has been ten days since I purchased the car and the problem list is extensive. It includes these problems:

— Cruise control varies up to 20 MPH from speed setting

— Left turn signal does not return to "off" after turn

— The stereo speaker on the right side door does not work

— The button to open the sunroof must be pressed several times before it opens, and

— The light in the glove box does not light up when open.

I plan to bring the car in for repair of these items on October 20. I expect all of these items to be repaired on that day. Please give these problems your personal attention to make sure all items are properly repaired.

Thank you.

Sincerely,

Unhappy With Lawn Maintenance

Dear Jose,

Please discontinue lawn service immediately.

Over the past several months, I have become very dissatisfied with your service. First of all, our agreement calls for service every other week. Sometimes you don't come for three or four weeks at a time. By that time, the grass is so long it's an eyesore to the neighborhood.

For the past two months you have been coming on Saturday while I'm away from the house. Your workers won't go in the backyard because of my dog. As a result, the backyard does not get cut.

Lastly, the vines on the front of the house are so long they are climbing onto the roof tiles, causing them to crack.

I don't know what happened, Jose, but I hope for your sake that your other customers are being better taken care of than me.

Sincerely,

Dissatisfied With Carpet Cleaning

Dear Mr. Martinez:

This letter is to inform you that I am not at all satisfied with the carpet cleaning services performed in my home on June 1.

After the workmen finished, the carpet had white streaks about three feet apart across the entire room. The workmen assured me the streaks would disappear once I vacuumed after the carpet dried in about 12 hours. Well, I vacuumed the carpet three or four times and the streaks are still there.

I called Nick Borrelli on the problem and he said he would send someone out to look at the carpet. It's been over a week now and no one ever came out. What really bothers me is that Mr. Borrelli has refused to return my calls.

I am really upset about the poor treatment I've received from Jimmy Clean Carpet Cleaners. I'm on the verge of filing a complaint with the City Consumer Protection Agency and the State Carpet Cleaners Association.

All this could be avoided by either refunding the $210 paid to you or sending someone out to remove the streaks.

I am awaiting your immediate action on this matter.

Sincerely,

Car Repair Not Done Properly

Dear Mr. Wilson:

On August 14, I took my car to your dealership because it was pulling to the right. The service manager said it needed a front end alignment. I approved the work at a cost of $73.

When I drove the car home from the dealership, it showed some improvement, but still pulled to the right.

On a hunch, I checked the air pressure in both front tires. The left read 35 PSI, the recommended pressure. But the right tire read 84 PSI, a dangerous level of pressure.

I believe one of your repairmen increased the pressure in the right tire in an effort to correct the pull to the right.

The manager of Bambibi's Tire Sales told me that at 84 PSI of pressure, the tire could explode, causing the driver to lose control of the car.

My wife routinely drives this car with my three-year-old twin daughters. And the stupidity of one of your repairmen could have easily caused the injury or even death of my family.

I am demanding you return the $73 paid to you for the "alignment." Don't force me to pursue this matter in the judicial system. Send the check to me at the above address.

Yours truly,

Letter Requesting Refund

Gentlemen:

Thank you for the opportunity to sample your diet pills on the 10-day free trial offer. While I found the pills satisfactory, they seemed to upset my stomach. As you will note, I am returning the product in its original carton, per your request.

Thank you again.

Cordially yours,

Chapter 25

Forms of Address

Occasionally, you may have reason to write a letter to a federal, state, municipal or school official. Listed below are the proper forms of address to use:

The President

The President
The White House
Washington, D.C. 20500

Sir:
My dear Mr. President:
Dear Mr. President:

Wife of the President:

Mrs. (Full Name)
The White House
Washington, D.C. 20500

Dear Mrs. _____ :

Forms of Address

The Vice-President

The Honorable (Full Name)
The Vice-President
  of the United States
Washington, D.C. 20501

Sir:
Dear Sir:
Dear Mr. Vice-President:
Dear Mr. _____ :

Senator

The Honorable (Full Name)
The United States Senate
Washington, D.C. 20510

Dear Sir (Madam):
My dear Senator _____ :
Dear Senator _____ :

Member of Congress

The Honorable (Full Name)
The House of Representatives
Washington, D.C. 20515

Dear Sir (Madam):
My dear Congressman
  (Congresswoman) _____ :
My dear Mr. (Madam) ___ :
Dear Mr. (Madam) _____ :

Cabinet Member

The Honorable (Full Name)
Secretary of (Department)
Washington, D.C. (Zip Code)

Dear Sir (Madam):
My dear Mr. (Madam) ___ :
Dear Secretary:
Dear Mr. (Madam) _____ :

**Chief Justice
of the United States**

The Honorable (Full Name)
Chief Justice
   of the United States
Washington, D.C. 20543

My dear Mr. Chief Justice:
Dear Mr. Chief Justice:

**Associate Justice
of the United States
Supreme Court**

The Honorable (Full Name)
Justice of the Supreme Court
   of the United States
Washington, D.C. 20543

My dear Mr. Justice:
Dear Mr. (Madam) Justice:

Governor

The Honorable (Full Name)
Governor of (name of state)
(state capital), State (Zip)

Sir (Madam):
Dear Sir (Madam):
Dear Governor _____ :
My dear Governor _____ :

Lieutenant Governor

The Honorable (Full Name)
Lieutenant Governor
   of (name of state)
(state capital), State (Zip)

Sir (Madam):
Dear Sir (Madam):
Dear Mr. (Madam) _____ :

State Senator

The Honorable (Full Name)
State Senator
(state capital), State (Zip)

Dear Sir (Madam):
Dear Senator ——————— :

**State Assemblyperson
(Legislature)**

The Honorable (Full Name)
State Assemblyman
    (Assemblywoman)
(state capital), State (Zip)

Dear Sir (Madam):
Dear Mr. (Madam) ——————— :

Mayor

The Honorable (Full Name)
Mayor of (City)
(Name of City), State (Zip)

Dear Sir (Madam):
Dear Mr. (Madam)
    Mayor ——————— :

City Councilperson

Councilman (Councilwoman)
    (Full Name)
City Hall
(Name of City), State (Zip)

Dear Sir (Madam):
Dear Mr. (Madam) ——————— :

Superintendent of Schools

Dr. (Full Name)
— or —
Mr. (Madam) (Full Name)
Superintendent of Schools
(Name of School System)
(followed by address)

My dear Dr. _____ :
My dear Mr. (Madam) ____ :

School Principal

Dr. (Full Name)
— or —
Mr. (Madam) (Full Name)
Principal of (Name of School)
(followed by address)

My dear Dr. _____ :
My dear Mr. (Madam) ____ :

School Teacher

Dr. (Full Name)
— or —
Mr. (Madam) (Full Name)
(Name of School)
(followed by address)

Dear Dr. _____ :
Dear Mr. (Madam) _____ :